TRELLIS

JAMIE GARNOCK

TRELLIS

The Creative Way to Transform Your Garden

Special photography by Hugh Palmer

With 190 illustrations and diagrams,
including 60 in colour

RIZZOLI
NEW YORK

A suggestion for a trellised winter garden from an Edwardian catalogue of garden ornament.

Frontispiece: *A finely trellised gazebo provides a major focal point on the long axis of a flower garden.*

First published in the United States of America in 1991 by Rizzoli International Publications, Inc.
300 Park Avenue South, New York, NY 10010

Specially drawn illustrations by Annick Petersen

ISBN 0–8478–1428–9
LC 91–52836

Printed and bound in Italy

CONTENTS

INTRODUCTION

Architectural features in landscape design have been used for over four thousand years to both practical and decorative effect. While the fundamental purpose of such features may have remained constant, their design, style and creation have all been subject to change and modification according to their period. Of all the embell-

ishments brought by man to his planned landscapes and gardens, trellis-work has proved an architectural effect of the utmost versatility, evolving from its agrarian origins around 2000 B.C. to a diversity of forms in many different societies. As a practical aid, providing support and shelter, enclosure and definition, its flexibility has been incomparable. In its more elaborate forms, however, trellis has taken on a more decorative aspect, sometimes belying its practical functions. Whether functional, decorative, or both, it can express simple restraint or subtle suggestion as well as extrovert, grandiose drama. It can articulate Gothic, Palladian and Rustic styles, and portray Oriental, Islamic and Moorish moods. Helped by royal patronage in seventeenth-century France, trellis reached such ambitious heights of unbridled showmanship that the term *treillage* was coined, as distinct from the simpler *treillis* or lattice. As terms of reference, the

Trellis can be divorced entirely from its practical function. This colourful contemporary example (left) shows how trellis can provide exciting decoration in any space, even when it is not combined with planting.

Originally developed as support for vines four thousand years ago, trellised pergolas can also be used to create cool, shady areas within a garden. At Biltmore, North Carolina (right), the garden created for the Vanderbilt family in the 1890s includes a spectacular tunnelled pergola. Windows, reminiscent of seventeenth-century Dutch pergolas, have been cut into the diamond-mesh panels to frame views of scenes beyond; the combination of architectural pattern and planting throws a tapestry of shadows along the whole length of the pergola.

distinction remains, *treillage* suggesting an art form in its own right.

Of all man's architectural endeavours in the landscape, trellis has also been the one to have reached furthest into the realms of pure horticulture. Quite apart from its constant use in fruit and kitchen gardens, it has been associated with plantsmanship and, most notably, the centuries-old cultivation of the rose.

While few other forms of garden ornament and embellishment can claim such comprehensive and universal usage, the life of any trellis is frustratingly short, apart from that constructed in metal. The inherent delicacy of a latticed design and, more especially, the susceptibility to outdoor elements of its most common medium – thinly carpented wooden slats – can be aggravating to the gardener and disappointing for the historian. Stone features of the Emperor Hadrian's garden survive from 1800 years ago, but we only have documentary evidence of French wooden *treillage* of two hundred years ago.

Modern techniques are now available for the better preservation and maintenance of wood, but the lifespan of trellis remains short compared with other architectural materials. However, in demanding frequent replacement, trellis has been able to respond more closely to movements of fashion. Compared with urns and statues, it is perhaps a better barometer of architectural style within the landscape.

The development of European and American trellis-work has always been subject to foreign influence, the movement of armies, missionaries and traders being as significant to the dissemination of ideas as the later travels of articulate observers, such as the eighteenth-century architect Sir William Chambers. Islamic and Moorish influences were felt first, followed by free interpretations of Chinese styles. The impact of Japanese and Shinto traditions were the last to arrive, delayed until the nineteenth century. European trellis-work has regularly displayed a curiosity for such new ideas, especially from the Orient, where the conceptual approach to lattice pattern is significantly broader. Contemporary Oriental styles continue to offer Western tastes an approach to pattern that is refreshing in its sophistication.

It would be wrong, incidentally, to attribute the origins of trellis exclusively to parallel developments in Europe and Asia.

In 1519, Cortes arrived at the royal gardens of Iztapaplan in Mexico and found paths flanked with trellis on which shrubs and climbers were grown.

A word should be added here about the terminology of trellis-work structures. Confusion exists over the distinction between terms such as 'pergola', 'arbour', 'bower' and 'gazebo'. While acknowledging that certain ambiguities of usage exist, I intend to follow the definitions given below for the purposes of this book.

'Pergola' comes from the Latin *pergula* which referred to a projecting roof (and, incidentally, a brothel). More significant is the derivation from the Latin word *pergere* to go straight through, to proceed with to an end – which gave rise to various derivations in Latin languages suggesting movement forward and thus the pergola will refer to structures designed for progression rather than rest. A 1675 definition of pergola mentions a covered walk formed of growing plants over trellis-work. The extent to which planting was sometimes encouraged led, as in many seventeenth-century Dutch gardens, to so much enclosure that the word *tonnelle* became more appropriate.

English commentators have referred to the Dutch *tonnelles* as tunnelled arbours, and indeed 'arbour' also describes trees and shrubs trained on trellis-work. Its derivation is more oblique, coming from a muddle between the Latin word *arbor*, for a tree, and the word *herba*, young plant, from which was derived the medieval *herbarium*, the *hortus conclusus*, which often included trellis-work. The arbour, however, while still incorporating an overhead structure and planting, is closely associated with the English word 'bower' and the French *berceau*, *cabinet de verdure* and *retraite*. All suggested a place for rest and contemplation. In their invitation to stop rather than move there is a useful distinction between the arbour and the onward mood of the pergola. It is worth noting that *berceau*, in French literature, while usually referring to an arbour, was also used to denote a vault-shaped trellised structure, *berceau* in French architectural terminology referring to a vault.

The 'gazebo' is either as a diminution of 'gaze about' or, as widely suggested, facetious Latin for 'I will gaze'. It refers to open-sided structures that were originally designed for admiring the view.

This project for the corner of a heavily planted garden (opposite above), shows trellis in two of its major roles: as highly decorative perimeter fencing and as an architectural backdrop to foreground planting.

Trellis can almost always serve a practical need in an elegant and stylish fashion. The soaring end-piece (opposite below), with its magnificent proportions and balance, does more than conclude a small urban garden: it also serves as the façade of a potting shed.

Style and detail in this perimeter trellis (below) brings the essential ingredients of seclusion and shelter to an overlooked terrace garden. A well-scaled and beautifully carpented display of contrasting pattern, arches, finials and broken pediment provide character and welcome relief from the surrounding skyline.

THE VARIETY OF TRELLIS

Trellis is one of the most versatile types of garden ornament; it may be used in simple, practical structures, or to achieve complex and decorative architectural effects as in this aviary in an English garden.

ORIGINS AND THE ANCIENT WORLD

This fresco in a villa at Pompeii (opposite), illustrates the increasingly sophisticated use of trellis-work in the gardens of the Roman era as they must have been at the time of the destruction of the city in A.D.79. Diamond-mesh patterns were common, though most, unlike this structure, had only minimal structural support. Here, where the planting becomes larger and wilder beyond the screen the trellis is typically used to define and compartment different areas and uses.

The original impetus for the development of trellis-work was the grape. Around 2000 B.C. vines were an important crop for the Hittites and Egyptians and it was noted that they grew more vigorously if supported. Trailing laterals could be held by simple frames of wooden mesh. Furthermore, if the structure was angled over in the shape of a projecting roof, not only could more vine be trained and cropped but a welcome area of shade resulted underneath. The earliest trellis thus took the form of crude pergolas and arbours, primarily for husbandry, but also for shelter from the elements.

For as long as the communities within those Hittite and Egyptian societies were scattered, sturdy and impenetrable barriers were needed to protect their houses and crops against perils. With time, however, communities akin to fixed villages evolved. The perimeter of a village required proper protection, but barriers between the individual properties could be fashioned with less material and lighter designs. The lattice fence was quick and easy to construct and, though not a complete deterrent, its distinct definition was (and remains) vital.

These communities saw the plot around the house not as a field but a garden in which various needs had to be met. Having defined its external boundaries, there was a wish to design and sub-divide the area within, according to purpose. Low and attractive diamond-mesh fences delineated orchards, herbs, vines and pools of water. The trellis on pergolas and arbours also, in closer communities, offered privacy and seclusion, and in serving such human pleasures they began to attract carpented and painted embellishment. Increasing levels of sophistication and need prompted further developments. In Persia, notably, heavy and dense diamond-mesh panels were employed to enclose garden compartments. Shade and privacy were of course useful, but more significant was the aspiration for a secluded 'paradise' ('paradise' deriving from the Persian word *pairidaeza*).

Ideas gravitated westwards, to be assimilated first by Greek society and then by the Romans. Early records from Pompeii's Samnite gardens (200–100 B.C.) and villas of the Roman Empire depict garden compartments unfolding between lattice fencing and pergolas. By the second century A.D., the Emperor Hadrian was commissioning trellised arbours for his villa at Tivoli (his hope being that their design would resemble the lines of masonry). This early attempt at a *trompe-l'oeil* illustrates the increasing demands made of trellis-work. His intention was that the arbours, similar to those in Pliny the Younger's gardens, would be festooned with roses (not vines). Pliny's theories on garden design welcomed trellis for both aesthetic and practical reasons. He was fascinated by the juxtaposition of architecture and nature, designing 'open' gardens (as they became known) towards the end of the first century A.D. at his villas at Laurentum near Rome and Tifernum Tibernium in Tuscany. Thus he revelled in the possibilities of trellis-work generally and the trellised arbour specifically. Influenced by the interest in horticulture of his uncle and adopted father, Pliny the Elder, Pliny the Younger also valued trellis for the presentation of plants and seasonal effects, and most especially for the display of roses. One of his letters describes episodes along a cypress flanked *allée* at his Tuscan Villa: 'Roses also grow there making this sunlit area a delightful contrast to the freshness of the shadows'.

Trellis was now a conscious part of urban and suburban fashion, and the cultural influence of the Roman Empire across the rest of Europe was to disseminate it as such. It had evolved a long way from being a simple agrarian device. The construction of the trellised arbour in Roman times accounts for the derivation of the word trellis. Referred to as *trilicius*, 'tri' was a thread and 'licium' a warp, and it was thus that the joints of the pattern were secured. This method is still used in the East.

MIDDLE AGES AND RENAISSANCE

A scene from the 1499 edition of the influential Hypnerotomachia Poliphili (below) *illustrates a notable feature of the medieval and Renaissance garden, namely the pursuit of pleasure within the seclusion of a trellised enclosure.*

Despite the lapse of a thousand years, Roman concepts remained the starting point for the medieval garden, the Dark Ages having arrested any intervening development. Enclosure was still sought for security and demarcation, but was more notable for its seclusion, the garden increasingly an open-air room devoted to the pursuit of pleasure.

The Renaissance mind took considerable pride in the design of gardens. Symmetrical and ordered, it relied on low trellis fences for concise division and sub-division, and larger trellised structures for arbours and

pergolas. Contemporary artists record numerous activities within the garden's compartments, from conversation and *alfresco* meals, to poetry, reflection, romance and chivalry. The *hortus conclusus* was also symbolic of the Virgin Mary, the intimate enclosure representative of her sanctity and its plants flourishing in recognition of her virtue. Trellis enabled further allusion to this much revered figure by supporting the roses with which she was associated.

The internal lattice fence was certainly a distinctive feature of these gardens. Almost all (according to artists) appear to have been carefully designed, combining a choice of square- and diagonal-mesh with a choice of finishes, paints (usually green) being often preferred to 'natural' wood. Though normally a metre or less in height, taller sections of fencing were employed where a seat might otherwise be overlooked.

The trellis panels were invariably complemented by elegantly proportioned and attractively detailed posts and rails. Some were overtly ornate, others incorporated carved animals and heraldic devices. The rails were also fashioned to arch over entrances. While most trellised enclosures displayed a delightful combination of artistry and restraint, heavily embellished and architectural structures began to appear in France during the sixteenth century, pointing the way to future developments there within the formal tradition.

Trellis was extensively used in Renaissance Europe for pergolas, tunnels and arbours. The arbour, especially, was seen as vital to any garden and worthy of obvious styling. Pergolas and tunnels were open on one side (like monastic cloisters), being referred to as 'galleries'. All three forms inspired differing levels of design and purpose, some short and simple, others enclosing garden compartments around all four sides. Their roofs were predominantly rounded and arched.

If trellised fences were planted at all, red and white roses and carnations were popular, while irises, marigolds and columbines were also used. Arbours were heavily planted with roses, honeysuckle, fruiting and ornamental vines, hops, and even bindweed. On the larger structures, planting was invariably subject to pruning and shaping. Trellis could also be purely horticultural, supporting fruit trees, vines and herbs. While normally vertical in such

roles, trellis was also laid horizontally over beds, or in a tubular fashion around pots, especially during the vogue for carnations, which combined well with low trellis.

Iron was occasionally used for the uprights of trellised structures, notably in Renaissance Italy. However, wood (especially willow, hazel and juniper) was plentiful and easily carpented for use in a whole variety of constructions. Trellised fences, arbours and pergolas became, throughout Europe, a common feature in all gardens, whether religious or secular, large or small.

In a setting typical of many medieval gardens (below), Henri of Navarre is seen in this 1526 miniature within a compartment enclosed by low trellised fencing contemplating a marguerite daisy. The trellis-work is supported by properly carpented and pleasantly proportioned uprights, finials and rails.

THE FORMAL TRADITION

Trellised porticoes were a popular focal point of seventeenth-century Dutch gardens. The design (above), from J. van der Groen's Den Nederlandtsen Hovenier (1669), illustrates the restraint which was often apparent in the Dutch interpretation of the French-led vogue for treillage.

From the same source comes this design for a tunnelled pergola; such structures became increasingly fashionable in the seventeenth-century Dutch garden as surrounds for the various compartments of the garden.

Northern Europe

The Dutch gardens of the seventeenth century were perhaps of greater practical influence than the showmanship of French design. They combined Italian classicism with elements of contemporary French fashion, but articulated the whole (if not all the parts) with a sense of intimacy and restraint that reflected the bourgeois patronage of Holland's wealthy and prestigious merchants. This appealed especially to those countries where cultural aspirations were relatively free of royal extravagance.

Enclosures remained popular, the Dutch excelling in their potential for architecture. Galleries were replaced by tunnels, constructed in the style of densely trellised pergolas. The trellis-work was vital but ultimately unseen, enabling thick planting using elms, limes, privet and other plants to be sculpted into solid shapes. Tunnels defined areas within the garden, surrounded parterres and pools, and ran parallel to garden canals. Many profiles were particularly dramatic; most had arching roofs, while some – Zorgvliet being a splendid example – flaunted windows

and peaked or domed pavilions on corners. Trellis was also employed unseen to provide more intimate structures such as small arboured recesses in the style of arch-topped sentry boxes.

Arbours, porticoes and arches, a common feature of Dutch gardens and their canals, were often constructed of quite elaborate *treillage*, deliberately eye-catching in both design and finish (blue and blue-green paints being popular). Their inspiration was French, as sometimes were their craftsmen. Louis XIV's Revocation of the Edict of Nantes in 1685 forced Daniel Marot (1661–1752) to the Netherlands. Marot contributed to gardens such as Het Loo, Zeist and de Voorst and his schemes were echoed abroad in English, Flemish and German gardens.

One specifically Dutch contribution to the architecture of *treillage* was the obelisk. Painted white and strategically sited to flank, punctuate or close vistas, obelisks provided the vertical focus that the naturally flat landscape lacked. These, and other popular styles of trellis, were illustrated in J. van der Groen's influential *Den Nederlandtsen Hovenier* (The Dutch Gardener) of 1669, a hugely successful book which was reprinted in several editions, including French and German, until well into the eighteenth century.

Dutch ideas and publications spread across northern Europe via the trading routes along which her merchants were so active. For England, however, an even closer link was forged when William and Mary came over from the Netherlands in 1688 to succeed James II. Both were very keen gardeners, familiar with all the latest Continental fashions and fresh from their own improvements at Het Loo. With them were courtiers such as Bentinck, who had transformed his garden at Zorgvliet. English garden design in the seventeenth century had been slow to evolve from the Renaissance format; potential patrons had been distracted by decades of civil, political and religious turmoil. Under the new Dutch influence at court, however, much needed improvements to gardens and their trellised structures were adopted, the Dutch approach being especially acceptable in the English context. At the same time, the more elaborate French style was becoming familiar, partly through John James' 1712 translation of D'Argenville's *La Théorie et la pratique du jardinage*.

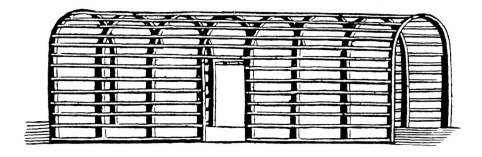

France and Spain

The pride in design and love of device that had characterized Renaissance gardens achieved their apogee in France, laying the foundations for the *treillage* of the seventeenth and eighteenth centuries. This was to be one of the most enduring traditions of trellis-work. As early as the 1390s, gardens such as the Jardin du Champ-au-Plâtre at the royal Hôtel-de-Saint-Pol in Paris included an array of trellised pavilions and *tonnelles*. The ubiquitous arbour was, by 1572, less concerned with intimacy; the confines of the medieval garden fell from favour as views of the surrounding landscape became fashionable. Degrees of enclosure were still required, however, and throughout the centuries trellis remained a vital prerequisite for sculpted planting, enabling the creation of *bosquets*, *berceaux* and *tonnelles*.

Against the larger perspective of the post-Renaissance garden, however, trellis design required greater architectural presence if it was to impress. Trellis-work adopted Palladian styles and was subject to ever increasing proportion and complexity.

The seventeenth century saw *treillage* at its height, the show-piece being the gardens at Versailles. Some of the great provincial châteaux also boasted outstanding examples, especially Chantilly where, as well as the Maison de Sylvie, the Temple de l'Amour exhibited such sophistication that every architectural effect was reproduced in trellis, from its dome and cupola to finials in the style of urns. Versailles' gardens, however, ruled supreme, serving personal ambition and diplomatic propaganda. Every sort of trellised artistry was present, from the sculpted *bosquets* around the Bassin de Flore and the panels in the Colonnade, Salle de Bal and L'Ençelade to the grand *treillage* of the Trianon de Porcelaine.

To the French mind, these gardens embodied the power of man over nature and France over Europe, and they were indeed influential amongst kindred spirits. In Spain, early in the eighteenth century, the king, Philip V, commissioned equally spectacular *treillage* arcades and *allées* at Aranjuez. Similarly grand were some of the structures in the Buen Retiro in Madrid. The Moorish influence in Spain, however, was also felt and at Aranjuez, for instance, diamond-mesh panels were carpented

Before the end of the sixteenth century, Pierre le Nôtre's trellised designs showed the advanced state of French treillage compared with the rest of Europe. During the seventeenth and eighteenth centuries, almost every architectural effect was demanded of the leading treillageurs. At Chantilly, for instance, the Temple de l'Amour (left) achieved an astonishing level of grandeur and detail, including trellis-work finials in the style of urns.

The arches and diagonal trellis-work that surrounded so many Islamic courtyards and gardens remained a feature of Moorish design in Spain. At the Alhambra, the famous Patio de los Arrayanes (below) echoes this traditional effect in its stone- and tile-work.

with small semi-circular windows. Trellis did not fire the imagination in Italy as it did elsewhere, the only good example of eighteenth-century *treillage* being at the Villa Crivelli Sormai-Verri and that was designed by a French *treillageur*.

Treillage remained popular in France throughout the eighteenth century, inspiring more diverse forms. The optical illusions created with carpented *trompe-l'oeils* were popular, sometimes accompanied by *trompe-l'oeil* paintings to heighten the effect. Preceding Repton's trellis-edged 'flower baskets' at the end of the century, the French developed the *corbeille* to surround planting. One design describes an ebony plinth (just above ground level), chestnut lattice (dense diamond-mesh overlain with verticals), oak struts and an oak rim. The glorious magic of seventeenth-century *treillage* was sometimes lost in over-elaboration in the eighteenth; except in the traditional garden pavilion.

The false perspective of trellised trompe-l'oeils was just one of the elaborate devices used in French treillage. The example (opposite) at Château de Brécy is thoughtfully sited; the stonework and clipped planting into which the trellis is recessed enhance the illusion.

This rose-festooned corner arbour at Villandry (below) is a twentieth-century recreation of a seventeenth-century model.

THE LANDSCAPE TRADITION

The Picturesque approach to English garden design often included trellis-work as an incidental detail of garden buildings, as in William Kent's arbour at Rousham (below), Batty Langley advocated a marriage of English landscape principles and the French style of treillage (below right).

Early in the eighteenth century, the English began to question the validity of the grand effects of the French formal garden and the elaborate structures of its Dutch counterpart. What right did man have to contort nature with such arrogance? And what, anyway, was the need of man's insensitive artifice, given nature's inherent beauty? Amongst garden designers and

their prominent patrons (mainly large landowners) the waning popularity of the Continental set-piece was further encouraged by other factors. Improving agricultural practice was bringing about the transformation of sweeping tracts of otherwise unkempt countryside; and architectural fashion in the shires had turned from Gothic and Jacobean detail to the easy ('natural' to some minds) proportions of Palladianism.

William Kent (1685–1748), allegedly inspired by the pastoral scenes in the paintings of Claude and Poussin, replaced rigid formality with lines that flowed effortlessly across the view. 'Capability' Brown (1716–83) went further, his landscapes taking in the immediate vicinity of any building in the belief that nature was itself a garden, the two being synonymous.

To this end, subtle contrivances, such as ha-has, were still needed, but trellis was effectively banished to the kitchen garden. Its laboured pattern was too reminiscent of man's arrogant disregard for natural form. Amongst devotees of the Picturesque, trellis found little favour but it did maintain a presence. Their interpretation of the English landscape style sought Classical, Gothic

Shady walks with Temples of Trelliss work after the grand manner at Versailes

and Oriental structures as unobtrusive ingredients of the larger scene. As with Kent's Classical seats at Rousham (from which the landscape could be admired), and especially within the increasing vogue for *chinoiserie* and the Rustic, trellising was a subsidiary but vital component.

More ambitious was the rear-guard action in the first half of the eighteenth century against the pure English landscape style. Batty Langley (1696–1751) advocated a marriage between the main features of French formalism and the more relaxed style of the English designers. He committed his hopes to print in his 1728 publication, *New Principles of Gardening*, suggesting gloriously ornate *treillage* amongst ha-has, countryside and wilderness. In England there were few adherents for so obvious and instant a hybrid. On the Continent, however, garden design allowed its native pride for *treillage* to combine with a fashionable curiosity about the *jardin anglais*. At Chantilly and Versailles, *jardins anglais* were added as subsidiary compartments to formal schemes, while at Haga in Sweden, Piper's full English Landscape for King Gustavus III included details such as Gjörwell's elaborate *salon de treillage*.

Humphrey Repton

Humphrey Repton's life (1725–1818) coincided with a period of profound social change. This saw a massive growth in Britain's wealth and an accompanying rise in the fortunes of the middle class and minor gentry. Unlike 'Capability' Brown, whose work had been for the larger landowners, Repton often found himself involved with the garden aspirations of the newly prosperous. Wealth and expectation were focusing on landscapes of smaller dimensions, the ideal arena for the versatility of trellis. In Repton's designs, then, it was gradually returned to prominence, perhaps festooned with roses, arching over paths, or dividing and sub-dividing enclosures; it covered orangeries, greenhouses, verandahs, loggias and even poultry houses; it roofed over areas in the form of arbours and framed views.

There are many fine records of Repton's trellis-work. The 1812 *Red Book* for Sheringham is typical. It records a scene from the proposed flower garden, which, at first sight, seems in the mood of a design by Brown, with no hint of a garden in the

Repton's skill at combining trellised effects and wider landscape effects was considerable. His 1813 design for Ashridge (below), with its elegant and airy arcade, fanning patterns, open arches and low trellised fence, anticipates the nineteenth-century mania for rose gardens.

Another fine example of the finesse with which Repton employed foreground trellis to serve as a flowing prelude to the view of a 'natural' landscape beyond in his 1805 design for White Lodge in Richmond Park (above). Repton here conceived a series of trellised arches and pillars to flank the symmetry of the path and architecture of the house.

naturally rolling ground. Lifting the movable flap on the relevant watercolour in the *Red Book*, a very different foreground appears, although a view of the wider panorama is still preserved. The new flower garden is surrounded by a waist-high lattice-work fence reminiscent of the Renaissance garden. Within are beds with trellised 'flower basket' edges (he first used them at Courteenhall in 1791, employing a more open pattern than the French), an orangery decorated with diamond and square-mesh patterns finished in 'Repton

Blue' and, to achieve a balanced effect, an arched arbour. The latter is in green *treillage* with two trellised wings in similar style, each with five arches, square-mesh cornice, and diamond-mesh balustrading to echo the perimeter lattice fencing. The wings stretch out six or more metres on each side of the arbour, at least two and a half metres high, gently curving back towards the centre of the garden, before terminating in square pillars of diamond-mesh and Classical pediments. Such a proposal was a dramatic departure from the Brownian tradition,

though still fairly conservative compared to the French styles.

Repton had a wide appreciation of different styles of trellis, from Moorish to Rustic, and their application to the detail of almost anything on which he focused. (He advocated, incidentally, the heavier construction of trellis in the French manner.) Responding to the new fashion for roses, Repton firmly established the use of trellised arcades, pillars and columns. All aimed to create a foreground over which the eye would be guided to the countryside beyond.

Orientalism

Although trellis and *treillage* in England had to wait for Humphrey Repton before once again becoming an important motif in garden design, the rise of Orientalism did provide it with an important stimulus. The English landscape style had advanced so far in little more than one generation that counter-revolution was inevitable. The eighteenth century was an age of change, where garden aspirations were being ex-

The enthusiasm with which chinoiserie was greeted in eighteenth-century landscape design encouraged the adoption of open lattice designs, as in this kiosk designed by Sir William Chambers (above). Such garden buildings were often finished in brightly coloured lacquers.

tended beyond the land-owing elite and where the spread of British overseas interests was awakening curiosity in other cultures.

The intriguing patterns of the Orient were a timely inspiration. The much travelled English architect, Sir William Chambers (having already explored Classical and Moorish influences in Europe) visited China in 1744 and 1748. Three influential publications resulted: *Designs for Chinese Buildings* (1757), *Plans, Elevations, Sections, and Perspective Views of the Gardens and Buildings at Kew in Surrey* (1763) and *Dissertation on Oriental Gardening* (1772). He delighted in challenging the severity of Brown's 'common fields' with *objets* such as the Chinese pagoda at Kew, with its nine storeys of red lacquer balconies and lattice.

The 'interpretation' of Chinese styles by Chambers, Chippendale (*The Gentleman and Cabinet-maker's Director* in 1754) and Charles Over (*Ornamental Architecture in the Gothic Chinese and Modern Taste* in 1758) accelerated a fashion for Oriental lattice patterns on a wide range of garden structures and furniture. William Newton, the Hiorn brothers, the Halfpennys and other designers, guided by the above publications, introduced *chinoiserie* trellis-work to pagodas, pavilions, kiosks, gazebos and bridges. Stylized buildings were, furthermore, a prompt for stylized furniture.

The clarity of the original Chinese concept was largely obscured in the interpretation; but the fashion thrived on hints of Eastern mystique, the impression of bamboo lattice (this was often faked as most of it was made from hardwoods, notably oak) and splashes of red lacquer and gilding.

'Chinese Chippendale' and *chinoiserie* have enjoyed waves of popularity ever since, both in Europe and especially in America, where it has been widely reproduced in its eighteenth-century form and exploited for its modern idiom.

Designers in the chinoiserie and Chinese Chippendale modes sometimes endowed their interpretations with an intensity of detail and contrast rarely seen in native Chinese models. The garden seat (opposite above right) incorporates a number of very attractive but startling designs.

While 'Capability' Brown deplored blatant contrivance in the landscape, his eighteenth-century critics delighted in the defiance offered by structures such as Sir William Chambers' 1757 Chinese pagoda at Kew (opposite left). Quite apart from its profile, its impact was heightened by ornate lattice work, painted in red lacquer, which decorated the balustrading of each ascending tier.

Chinoiserie and its accompanying lattice-work enjoyed a revival in the nineteenth century (left). Here, an open Chinese pagoda fountain (c. 1820) at Alton Towers, constructed in cast iron and beautifully scaled to its surroundings, has arches set in fish-scale patterned lattice.

THE GARDENESQUE AND RUSTIC

One of the principal achievements of John Claudius Loudon (1783–1843) was to place the display of plants and their husbandry at the forefront of English garden design. This 'gardenesque' style needed trellis, not as an architectural prelude to a view beyond, but as an indispensable support for climbers and shrubs. Under Loudon's powerful advocacy and the advent of horticulture as an industry, plantsmanship became fashionable. Anyone with a patch of ground and a few shillings to spare felt they could take part in this movement. 'Nature' and the 'landscape', in their broad eighteenth-century sense, were no longer a force; the garden, once again, was an enclosure, to be protected and planted. Trellis appeared everywhere, only to disappear under a jungle of growth, on internal and external boundaries, on the façades of houses (not always to architectural advantage) and other buildings and across the garden on arches and tripods. It was functional and unseen, 'garden design' being in the subsequent planting. Loudon's keen eye for plant performance prompted him to be specific about what should, and should not, be grown on various types of trellis. In his 1843 designs for the garden at Kiddington House in Oxfordshire the watercolour detail of proposed wall trellis is revealing. It illustrates thick climbers rendering the trellis invisible and describes how roses were not to be included because of their need for light and air. Wall trellis suited clematis, jasmine and honeysuckle, while free-standing trellis favoured roses.

Some stylised trellis was in use. The circular or gently curving rose arcade, with trellised arches, balustrading and pillars, remained popular. But they lost much of the Repton finesse, their proportions being heavier and more extravagant and their mood more enclosing.

Eighteenth-century rustic patterns, with trellising in uncarpented or rough-sawn wood (from yew, larch and fruit trees) also continued in vogue. They had long been either a deliberate or casual feature of garden seats and other *objets*, inspired by publications such as Robert Manwaring's *The Cabinet and Chairmaker's Real Friend and Companion* in 1765. Nature was mimicked in material, finish, and sometimes design with lattices of interlocking branches sprouting naturally from upright trunks. Repton and his son, John Adey, designed Swiss cottages and other buildings in the Rustic style, their pelmets and balustrades trellised accordingly. Greater flights of fancy were to come later, typified by the patterns illustrated in Shirley Hibberd's *Rustic Adornments for Homes of Taste* in 1856.

Rustic patterns for fencing, gates and hurdles, such as those of Papworth (opposite) explored a refreshing range of trellised designs and remained popular throughout the eighteenth and nineteenth centuries (see p. 28). Their artistry also provided a quiet outlet for Gothic styling.

Some rustic patterns were wrought entirely from natural forms, relying on the angular growth of yew and fruit trees. The trunks provided the uprights, while their branches produced the lattice, as in this garden building illustrated by Shirley Hibberd (below).

VICTORIAN AND EDWARDIAN TREILLAGE

The ubiquitous pergola of the Edwardian garden adopted either the pattern and ornamentation of Continental or Reptonian treillage or (below) the heavier and simpler lines of the English vernacular, as interpreted by Lutyens and the Arts and Crafts Movement.

One of the most influential books on the design of garden trellis in the nineteenth century was John Buonarotti Papworth's *Hints on Ornamental Gardening: consisting of a series of designs for garden buildings, etc.* (1823). Similar to Chippendale's *Director* 70 years earlier, this acted as a pattern book. The range of styles, many of them trellised, sought to be applicable to all tastes and situations. Papworth offered designs in wood as well as iron, continuing the eighteenth-century interest inspired by Tijou and Bakewell for wrought iron in the landscape. From charming Rustic panels in wood and flimsy arches to smartly painted

iron balustrading and *treillage*, trellis was available in all its forms.

The ranges of Papworth and others were not offered in response to personal commission but by advertisement. The success of this format was due to changes in technology, infrastructure and market demand. The development of cast iron, unlike the craftsmanship of wrought iron, suited mass-production and, though heavier and more fragile, could be produced more cheaply. Intricate detail was lost in the moulding process, but flowing patterns reproduced well. The advent of the railways enabled a wide distribution of centrally produced goods such as iron. And gardening was evolving as a mass pursuit.

One notable development of the period was wire trellis-work; it could be seen everywhere, especially in the form of arches, whose popularity was prompted by the mania for roses generally, and the 'rose garden' specifically. From magnificent show-piece parterres to humbler plots, the graceless wire arch could be seen the length and breadth of the country, usually supporting a profusion of planting. Wire trellis-work, however, was sometimes used to form more elaborate structures in the style of *treillage*. Arbours, aviaries and gazebos, some with Gothic arches and Moorish domes, were especially popular and often made conspicuous by their white painted finishes. Garden furniture and other ornament were also available in the style. One advantage of such ornament was that it was lightweight and transportable (some arbours were even set on wheels).

Wire trellis-work, very often in a quaint Gothic style, was also used around windows (both internally and externally), either free of planting or as part of the new fashion for window gardening. This was symptomatic of the Victorian craze for introducing horticulture to the house. Victorian gardening fashion was especially given to exotic displays of tropical planting and the joys of the conservatory (the development of the latter was aided by the capabilities of cast iron and, in Britain, the repeal of the Glass Tax in 1845). The aspirations of the indoor plantsman required an array of props and other paraphernalia to enable him to achieve the desired effects of cascading greenery. Trellis, either as a complete structure or as a decorative element of *jardinières*, was indispensable to such planting.

The later part of the nineteenth-century and the early part of the twentieth were marked by a revival of heavily styled trellis, which was now accorded an importance in landscape design reminiscent of Continental *treillage* two hundred years earlier. Inspiration, however, was drawn from a diverse range of historical, geographical and vernacular idioms, and the enthusiasm with which they were explored led to spirited debate on their relative merits. Rustic pattern was fused with Oriental intricacies; Gothic *treillage* encompassed elaborate *trompe-l'oeils*; Moorish and Palladian styles incorporated hints of the sudden vogue for Japanese design. Devey's designs for a *treillage* pavilion at Ascott House around 1880 offered his Rothschild client a triumphal arch of Palladian proportion with the choice of either heavy Classical detail or flowing *chinoiserie*. Just as remarkable for its Palladian grandeur was Guthrie's 1908 design for a summerhouse near Southampton which incorporated a large trellised dome supported by wooden columns on a simple, weather-boarded, one-storey building below. Other architects introduced lively mixtures of style to the lattice patterns of garden doors, gates and bridges.

To architects practising landscape design, the pergola was irresistible as a means of making the boldest statement of style. At Easton Lodge in Essex, for instance, Harold Peto installed a pergola of soaring grandeur and elaborate *treillage*. (Of interest, also, is the netting that was draped above its roof to stop the trailing stems of climbers from obscuring the architectural lines of structure.) Lutyens, on the other hand, reflected his advocacy of the Arts and Crafts Movement and its preoccupation with local skills and materials, and refused to indulge his numerous pergolas with the pattern that he sought in more durable mediums such as stone and brickwork. His wall trellis, also, was often bleak, heavily constructed and crude in profile, even when covered with Jekyll's profuse planting. The interest in the vernacular precluded the use of *treillage* as being too foreign, and Repton's style for being too sophisticated; both were, anyway, ill-suited to the architectural style of the Lutyens house.

The continuing enthusiasm and market for trellis in the Edwardian era, with all its excesses of style and combinations of pattern, is graphically illustrated by the catalogues from the Pyghtle Works of Bedford dating from the early years of this century. In oak, deal or teak, finished with oil, stain or paint, delivered in Britain or abroad, the Pyghtle Works offered fifty pages of *treillage* and trellis, with a further ten pages of pergolas and eight pages of bridges. From *treillage* temples, trellis pillars and fans (roses were sufficient excuse for *treillage* across Europe and America), to verandahs, porches, arbours, recesses and an exotic array of panels and arches, each design was confidently styled and named.

During the Edwardian era extensive catalogues began to offer ready-made trellis and treillage in revivalist styles. The 'Haarlem Arbour' (below right) offered by the Pyghtle Works was adapted from a seventeenth-century Dutch design (below left). Scale and finesse were, however, often forgotten in early twentieth-century design, as in this outsize and far from inviting 'arbour' (bottom).

CONTEMPORARY STYLES

Pure pattern is explored in these trellis-work wall sculptures by the innovatory English company of Thwaites and Pitt. With a purpose similar to the white obelisks of Dutch seventeenth-century landscape, the designs aim to provide sufficient focus and stimulation to lift the eye away from a bland backdrop.

Compared with other art forms available to the garden, trellis-work has not immediately established a popular modern idiom. Does the very definition of trellis, however, preclude it from innovatory concept? Have we, in fact, exhausted its permutations after 4,000 years? Or, as an architectural medium, does the evolution of trellis depend on the quality of attention paid to landscape design by practising architects? After all, their influence on garden design up to the 1930s had been considerable.

Fresh styles of trellis-work are nevertheless available from a number of innovative designers. In Europe and America, interesting variations on the Oriental disregard for dense repetition and monotonous predict-

ability have been produced. A Chinese influence can be found in some modern trellis screens, where the regular patterns are opened up by keeping repetition to a minimum, suggesting Chinese influence; others sound a Japanese note in the skilful coordination of varying densities.

Several modern suppliers now offer complete wall sculpture/trellis systems, consisting of a selection of basic components with the option of further elements tailored to an individual design; these can be used to create either free-standing or wall-mounted trellis-work. Pattern and profile can be dictated by owner and site, then refined by communication between owner and producer.

Trellis in the second half of this century, however, will be remembered more for a spirited reinterpretation of the traditional within the strictures of contemporary landscape manning and design. Trellised artistry is now often conceived for the smallest spaces and modest budgets, demanding imagination, restraint and subtlety in the reinterpretation of traditional forms, and inspiring a myriad of miniature and highly personal conceptions of paradise, some intense and complex, others brief and minimalist. Other fine examples of revivalist trellis have benefited from the cooperation of interior designers, especially in bringing pattern and proportion to small, otherwise uninteresting, areas.

Neo-classical in concept but entirely modern in mood, Thwaites and Pitt have produced a strong and cleverly scaled design (below) to transform the character of a foreground. The conviction with which this small scene is enclosed and concluded distracts the eye from the bleak setting beyond.

Gazebos continue to attract a fusion of styles; Artech, a London-based company making high-quality treillage, have here (left) combined Oriental allusion with modern detailing. The craftsmanship lends authority to this model.

This Thwaites and Pitt panel, while undoubtedly contemporary in expression, strikes a Japanese note in its dramatic variations of pattern, density and colour.

Also by Thwaites and Pitt is this novel design (right) based on a popular Chinese concept. Through the abbreviation and strategic omission of mesh, the lattice patterns appear to unfold, developing as they progress.

TRELLIS IN THE MODERN GARDEN

The modern garden is often seen as an outdoor 'room', compact in dimension and intense in purpose. Here, in a small city garden which leads on from the french windows of a sitting room, the ambience of a sunny conservatory has been sought through the effect of white diamond-mesh set against yellow walls.

ENCLOSURES AND EXTERNAL SCREENS

'Capability' Brown may have advocated a complete lack of enclosure, but his message was only acceptable to his clients because so many of them were the great Whig land-owners who owned and controlled much of what lay between their houses and the horizon. In these less spacious days, how-ever, the crucial and immediate challenge in the garden is the defence of one's own domain against the outside world, whether the community at large or, more specific-ally, the nearest neighbour.

Modern urban skylines are only too often the visual result of more and more people having to thrive and survive in less and less space. A setting may be dominated by high-rise buildings and industrial pressures; or it may be less conspicuous in profile but remain depressing in effect, with a pano-rama of uninspiring house and apartment fronts or, worse, the drab architecture and domesticity of their rears. Such back-drops to a garden can heavily modify the overall effect. And even country dwellers are not immune; rural scenes may be threatened by a new house or a pocket development, or by the increasing traffic and upgrading of local roads; nearby farmers may be erecting new buildings to farm more intensively or they may be diversifying out of agriculture into other enterprises.

The garden, however, is frequently the focus of expectations of finding an escape from the pressures of modern life. A mea-sure of privacy is therefore vital, even if it is sometimes only implied. The erection of solid barriers to a substantial height may appear the most logical way of achieving it.

The addition of low trellis to the top of a typical garden wall can transform the atmosphere of the space it encloses. As an external barrier, trellis cannot claim to be comprehensive, but as in this garden plan, it can provide a high degree of seclusion without being too oppressive.

Aesthetically, however, the creation of a total exclusion zone by high walls or fences can have its problems. Prisons, schools and other institutions may be justified in the building of such enclosures, but their concern is for function rather than atmosphere; garden owners who show a similar disregard for ambience in the pursuit of privacy may risk simply creating an oppressive space.

There are other factors that can dissuade us from lurking, like agoraphobes, behind huge barricades. High walls can be expensive; and high fences, apart from their expense, can be unwieldy and far from stable in strong winds. There may also be legal implications, either because planning per-

mission is required or because a neighbour's light is impaired.

Trellis is potentially one of the most useful forms of defence, reassuring in its architectural form, flexible in its dimension, but airy in substance and pattern. It can create – or, at the very least, suggest – an escape from the world beyond. When standing in the garden, perimeter trellising can form a new horizon, either in reality, where it supersedes the previous skyline, or by implication when it does not. Either way, the eye can be diverted or distracted.

The apparent isolation it affords can enable the most successful oases of elysian calm to flourish in some of the least promising settings. Congested city skylines and their sprawling surrounds can be artfully

lost behind clever trellising, as can the disconcerting proximity of next-door neighbours.

Trellis is typically seen providing the crucial few feet of extra protection above an existing wall or fence line. It not only promises, however, the extra height in a light, airy and attractive fashion, but also becomes the means of support for climbing plants as they move upwards. The result can be an effective and appealing screen, laden with foliage and flower and dappled with contrasting areas of light and shadow. As an external barrier, the combination of pattern, profile and function produced by climber-strewn trellis can boast a depth of interest which other forms of enclosure find hard to rival.

INTERNAL SCREENS

Decorative

Modern trellis-work draws its inspiration from a multiplicity of styles, many of which can be applied effectively to the reduced dimensions of today's gardens. One obvious source of inspiration is the Renaissance garden, which often had to be planned within a rigidly confined space without resorting to sweeping views of the landscape beyond.

The success with which the Renaissance gardeners brought together a series of component units into a single cohesive picture from which the outside world was excluded remains relevant today. Separate compartments within larger gardens can be created by using pleached trees, hedges and walls, but such methods would be wholly out of scale for most small gardens; it is here that trellis-work comes into its own. The possibilities are still enormous: trellis can be elaborate or subdued in style; it can be covered with a solid mass of clematis, roses and honeysuckle; or the planting can be minimal or even non-existent, allowing the lattice pattern to remain distinct with a view of adjacent scenes beyond.

The trellised fences of Renaissance gardens were all internal devices, dividing and sub-dividing larger areas for reasons of design, delineation and the creation of the ever important compartments, even with relatively low, lightweight and uncluttered lattice. Trellis-work can create and sub-divide areas with sensitivity and elegant understatement. Another source of inspiration and equally pertinent to the dimensions of many contemporary gardens (especially small terraces and patios, balconies and roof gardens) is the Japanese 'sleeve

Internal divisions in the garden can be marked with the lightest of trellis-work touches. In a style reminscent of Repton (above) corner fans of lattice bring movement to three elegant arches, concluding one area but immediately revealing the next.

Prior to planting with climbing hydrangeas and roses, these large trellised panels, inspired by Edwardian designs, soften the harsh lines of the tennis court beyond.

fence'. It can produce very effective division and interest, reaching up to six feet or more in height, but perhaps three feet or less in width.

Once divided by trellis, the garden is no longer a single scene to be absorbed at a single glance; it offers more intrigue and mystery, and enables a lot more composition and contrivance, amusing the owner and tempting the visitor. The definition given to separate areas within the whole can also be used to create or emphasize overall symmetry. Trellis that is purposefully oriented around internal compartments can also be positioned to guide the eye towards a strategic focal point beyond. In many urban gardens, the focal point itself often involves further trellis-work, perhaps in the form of a *trompe-l'oeil* or elaborate end-piece on a back wall.

Functional

The second significant motive for building trellised screens and compartments inside today's gardens is, like perimeter trellis, primarily defensive. It is not aimed against the outside world, however, but against the more unsightly artifacts of modern life.

Commonly sited within the confines of many gardens are such eyesores as dustbins, oil tanks, potting sheds, compost heaps, shelters for prams and bicycles, carports and garages. None are inherently attractive and most can bluntly disrupt the pleasant effects of the surrounding scenery (which may be the whole garden). Equally mundane and disruptive to the eye, despite their more leisurely connotations, are barbecues, sand pits, climbing frames, slides and children's play areas.

It is usually impossible to avoid glimpses of some or all of the above, even in more spacious gardens. It should, however, be possible to reduce a number, at least, to obscurity. Given the opportunities for pleasure that a garden should offer, eyesores should not be tolerated without attempting counter-measures. As with the neighbour or the building opposite, what one does not want to see can hopefully be transformed into something which, even at worst, no longer forces itself on the attention.

Trellis-work can be tailored to required dimensions and fixed so that, at a very small cost in terms of space, there is at least a lattice pattern immediately masking any-

thing that lies beyond. Uprights and trellis panels can surround oil-tanks and dust-bins; 'sleeve fence' panels can hide barbe-cues and sand pits. Patterns can be simple or eye-catching. Climbers can be employed; they might be evergreen, to cover some or all of the woodwork throughout the year; and even where there is no direct access to a bed, pots and tubs can be used.

Such decisions will depend upon whether one is seeking an anonymous effect that can sink discreetly into the back-ground, or whether the excuse for trellis-ing, albeit prompted by an eyesore, is also seen as an excuse for more elaborate effects.

Solid structures, such as garages, sheds and lean-tos, usually allow trellis to be fixed directly to an existing structure. Although offering significant improvement, the trellis could remain an incidental detail, its pre-sence cheerful and effective, but ultimately subservient. Lean-to structures, for in-stance, can benefit from simple trellised pelmets and supports. Alternatively, the trellis can be made into the dominant fea-ture of the whole structure. Some of the most improbable features and functions of the garden, including bicycle and potting sheds, have been masked with façades of gloriously misleading *treillage*.

This attractive open-work fencing not only distinguishes an orchard from a mown path, but also flanks a longer view. The eye is guided towards an inviting end-piece, itself heralded by trellised obelisks.

Protruding at right-angles from a wall (opposite) suitably styled panels can bring screening (in this case from a kitchen window), seclusion or interest to the smallest areas.

FREE-STANDING TRELLIS

Pergolas and Arches

Free-standing trellised structures in and around the garden have a long history, from the purely practical to the purely aesthetic, and every conceivable combination of both.

Pergolas represent one of the most ancient uses for trellising. Simple patterns in slats of wood were originally seen as being a cheap and effective way of producing a frame for climbing plants (especially vines), under which shade and shelter could be found. All over the world, such elementary structures remain widespread, constructed with crude lattice work and at low cost. As aspirations increased, and the designs for trellis evolved, arbours and pergolas were fashioned to suit higher purposes. The Renaissance and Dutch gardens were very often surrounded with pergola shaded walks. Generous planting with trees and shrubs, but strict training, produced a variety of sculpted effects, from galleries and cloisters to tunnels. They not only created sheltered walks but reinforced the effects of seclusion and intimacy in the area of the garden they enclosed, focusing the eye and the mind on the 'paradise' within rather than the world without. The intensity of composition and detail involved in today's small gardens, and the preponderance of unsympathetic skylines, warrants the continued use of pergolas as a deliberate instrument for creating enclosed effects. These effects can be reinforced by the extensive use of climbers. The *treillage* pergolas of seventeenth-century France and late-Victorian Britain have inspired only a minority following (partly because of the cost of reconstruction); and the compara-

The dimensions and continuous aspect of pergolas have traditionally attracted bold architectural effects and many late-Victorian and Edwardian designers were reluctant to see their designs obscured by excessive planting. Hence the obvious detail and craftsmanship involved in the pillars (above), the circular windows and arches (right) and the elaborate cross-pieces (far right).

This complex pergola (opposite above) shows the problems of a painted finish, especially if applied prior to the recent introduction of micro-porous paints; the application of fresh coats has to compete with established planting.

For at least two thousand years, arbours have combined the sense of retreat with every sort of artistry. Classical proportion and detail (opposite below left) are rendered less imposing by an arch cut into diamond-mesh trellis, the shadowy depths beyond imparting a sense of complete tranquillity and escape. Where space is at a premium in a small town garden (opposite below right) an abbreviated arbour might provide both a focal point and an invitation to rest.

The startling roof line and wide open diamond-mesh pattern of this gazebo (right) contrast sharply, in their white finish, with the subdued profile and tones of the trees beyond.

Set as an arbour, but with the open-sided spirit of a gazebo, the simplicity of this structure (below right) has been beautifully stage-managed.

Trellis can also convey an impression of sumptuous grandeur, as in the elaborate lines of this aviary (below).

tively severe lines of Lutyens' designs tend only to be echoed by architects working on modern commissions.

Over the last 300 years, but especially since the first part of this century, trellised pergolas and arches have been used along an important axis or sightline, their purpose being to draw the eye (and possibly the feet) towards the visual conclusion. In this role, contrasts of light and shadow, and the implication of distance, can be introduced to a view. The focus beyond can also be presented within (and set off by) the visual frame of the pergola or arch.

The arch, like the pergola, embodies movement and transition, tempting curiosity with the expectation of impending delights. This is regularly practised in every sort of landscape, but is especially appropriate in smaller gardens. A shrewdly positioned arch leading into an otherwise unseen area can suggest much more than may in fact exist.

Arbours and Gazebos

Arbours were considered a necessity in Roman and Renaissance gardens, where they provided a place for thoughtful repose; in many Victorian gardens they were seen as the opportunity for social intimacy and entertainment. Contemporary generations perhaps lack the time and the inclination to take their partners or their thoughts to a shady bower, but arbours are still popular for ornamental reasons. They can provide a delightful focus for a wider scene, or a conclusion to it, combining architecture and planting to create an atmosphere of escape and tranquility. A garden seat, flanked by trellised walls and partly shaded by climbers hanging from a solid or trellised roof overhead, is an attractive feature in its own right, especially against solid backdrops and profuse foliage. The feeling of peace which is so often associated with arbours explains the frequency with which they are offered in balanced Palladian styles.

The gazebo in the modern garden, like the arbour, is often used in a very different way from its predecessors in centuries gone by. Given the relatively restricted size of most modern gardens, gazebos are now rarely used as vantage points and are much more likely to be the focal point of a design and a useful area of shelter. In both its past and present roles, however, the gazebo tends to be seen as a place for activity rather than as a resting place within the garden. As such, many models tend to be more extrovert in pattern and detail than arbours, and less regularly shrouded in climbers and shadows. The need for a roof and uprights around four to eight otherwise open sides has given architects plenty of scope for exotic designs. Gothic arches, Moorish domes, pagoda canopies and *chinoiserie* have all been used, fashioned from wood, wire and other metals.

Both arbours and gazebos benefit from trellis-work; in turn, the pattern of the lattice is often effectively displayed in the context of such relatively small structures.

Obelisks, Tripods and Pillars

Vertical forms rising from any designed landscape carry authority and can almost be seen as an expression of man's domination of nature. Garden obelisks are architectural exclamation marks and invariably appear more dramatic in any garden than their 'green' equivalents such as clipped conifers.

The obelisk was developed for its visual effect by seventeenth-century Dutch gardeners; the flat contours of the land demanded the provision of as many points of interest as possible in garden design. It is the provision of vertical accent and interest which has ensured the continuing popularity of obelisks to this day, sometimes enlivening gardens considerably smaller than those Dutch ones. Twentieth-century garden design has used obelisks in symmetrical arrangements and also as a means of surprise and drama. Their visual impact, however, must be in keeping with the scale of the setting. Sharp, tapering lines and painted finishes, unless hidden under an untidy profusion of planting, perform like solo artists, rarely failing to draw the eye. Such prominence needs to dominate a proportionate amount of space and to be set off by a proportionate amount of contrast. The movement and drama embodied in an obelisk are most effective against a bland, composed background, hence their easy role in large herbaceous borders and vegetable gardens. Especially versatile in today's small garden is the

The profile of a trellised obelisk ensures that it is dramatic in effect even when simple in design (opposite above). More complex are these three designs (below) taken from seventeenth-century Dutch models. The Versailles tub (opposite below), a planter surmounded by a trellised obelisk, is especially useful in garden ornament.

Trellised pyramids (right) provide vertical accent in a garden but do not have the inherent panache of obelisks. Their squatter proportions are ideally blurred with profuse planting and as such they are an excellent aid to the plantsman.

obelisk which has a Versailles tub as its base (and means for planting) with a tapering trellis structure fitting on top. Beware the squatter shape of the pyramid. Vibrancy gives way to heaviness where the dimensions around the foot are too great for the overall height.

Trellised pillars and columns, festooned with roses and topped with plinths and finials, are reminiscent of Repton and the subsequent widespread fashion that swept Victorian Britain and America. They embody the same vertical emphasis, but their right-angled and proportioned profiles suggest a measure of decorum. The trellised pillar does not have the extrovert panache of the obelisk. It is less comfortable performing a solo role, preferring to be part of a larger pattern. Pillars are excellent in support of other features such as trellised panels or overhead structures, or as part of a free-standing series. Parallel, or near parallel, vertical lines that terminate too abruptly can produce anti-climax. To complete the profile, capping pieces, plinths and finials are often appropriate.

The richness of pattern and detail on the corner-pieces and columns of this pavilion (left) are reminiscent of the Rococo euphoria of mid eighteenth-century Europe.

This superb Gothic fantasy (opposite) erupts dramatically out of a flowing landscape, the shadow of its pair falling across the smooth mown grass in the foreground. In a colour that was popular for trellis in sixteenth- and seventeenth-century England, the scale, pattern and detail of the structure dominate the garden; Gothic styling is especially well-suited to such exuberant effects.

TREILLAGE

Fantasies

Any trellis-work which is more architectural than horticultural in purpose is expressing a greater or lesser degree of fantasy. Even in its use to define external and internal boundaries it implies a greater degree of separation and enclosure than it in reality provides. Mild but effective illusion is similarly derived from trellis by interior designers, especially on commercial premises such as restaurants, where larger areas are transformed with sub-division and contrived seclusion.

Trellis can also express more specific fantasy, suggesting ages, places or contexts which may be far removed in actuality from the site of the structure. Such statements are sometimes more than a simple indication of visual preference or sentiment; they can also reflect philosophical or personal need. The Persians wanted their gardens to be representations of 'Paradise', the Renaissance garden owners sought symbolic parallels to the Virgin Mary and the Garden of Eden. The great Continental *treillage* of the seventeenth century, though a striking sight, was a loud declaration of man's dominance of nature; while the extravagant styles of the nineteenth century expressed general feelings of superiority and self-confidence. Oriental patterns have explored the relationship of man and nature from a different angle, their designs, often of limited dimensions, being a deft embodiment of both meaning and fantasy.

The level of visual suggestion inherent in trellised styles remains a fascinating aspect of landscape design in an age where so much is expected of the garden, however small or unpromising the prospect. The scale and budget of today's gardens,

Trellis panels frame and flank a Gothic arch and mirrored trompe-l'oeil, the illusion suggesting that the trellis is merely separating one compartment from another area of the same garden beyond. The power of suggestion will improve as the jasmine matures to soften the abrupt impact of the wall.

however, requires an Oriental subtlety of approach, combining exactitude with a shrewd judgement of proportion and complementary planting. The smaller garden is similar to the smaller stage. Everything is closer and subject to a more intimate scrutiny than is possible with the grander panorama. On the other hand, the small stage is perfectly balanced by fantasy on a small scale. Ambitious sweeps of *treillage* only achieved their impact with more man-hours and acres than are easily afforded today. The scale of the modern garden allows a low budget creation to be produced with total conviction.

Seventeenth-century French *treillage* derived much of its effect from cocking a defiant snook at nature's supposed supremacy. The daunting conditions that surround many modern gardens beg similar acts of defiance. Current fashion, furthermore, sanctions style in any format. Thus, in the creation of today's trellised fantasy, there is both wide personal choice and availability. Moorish end-pieces, with arches and close-set diamond-mesh panels, look charming on paved or tiled gardens and roof terraces. Classical seats, in the style of William Kent at Rousham, with their pediments and trellised sides, can be tucked into shrubberies. Gothic panels with tapering finials can excite and lift what would otherwise be a bland piece of landscaping. *Chinoiserie* can refresh and the Japanese 'sleeve fence' might intrigue. For a late nineteenth-century feel, bold *treillage* with a profusion of climbing roses would be appropriate. And what could be more charming than a reproduction of the simple elegance and finesse of Repton's flowing designs.

Trompe-l'oeils

There can be no more obvious or far-fetched a fantasy than the false perspective effects of the *trompe-l'oeil*. The very form of trellis patterning lends itself to optical illusion and, as such, is an amusing device in an age where maximum effect is often expected from minimum dimensions. Trellised *trompe-l'oeils* are usually end-pieces to a view (however short), hoping to take the eye on beyond the reality of the actual confines, suggesting a distance that does not exist. Rather than being flat panels set

across a view, some illusory trellis runs (almost) parallel with a line of sight, flanking it on both sides, and introducing a false sense of distance to the middle ground through diminishing proportions and tapering width.

As with all illusions, some subtlety may be required for the deception to carry sufficient conviction. Complete deception is usually out of the question, but it is not essential where the potency and presence of the *trompe-l'oeil* induces a feeling of breadth. Such artifices can be used to break up the heavy effect of masses of masonry. The Emperor Hadrian hoped to achieve the opposite effect with trellis designed to resemble the reassuring solidity of masonry within a natural backdrop.

The standard *trompe-l'oeil* is an endpiece that portrays a pergola walk running away from the viewer and beyond which, close to eye-level, lies a horizon and vanishing point. The perspective of a garden can thus be lowered, away from the real skyline above. To give the illusion maximum emphasis, the pergola usually appears in the form of a seventeenth- or eighteenth-century *tonnelle*, the all-enclosing structure allowing a concentrated pattern with which to define its imaginary shape and onward passage.

Being the most unashamed sleight of hand, *trompes* invariably need more than clever carpentry to prevent them from appearing as laughable and hopeless contrivances. It is not uncommon to see a trellised *trompe-l'oeil* handled clumsily, itself appearing every bit as abrupt as the wall it may be attempting to hide. Without necessarily embarking on elaborate choreography, basic stage-management should give the illusion some sort of cohesion with its immediate surroundings.

Make sure that the immediate backdrop against which the pattern of the *trompe* is seen does not blatantly and instantly neutralize the false perspective. Some of the best examples of unnecessary and irritating competition between trellis and background are found with *trompe-l'oeils*. The ambitious perception that the trellis is trying to convey lacks all conviction if immediately undermined by the uncompromising and contradictory perspective embodied in a brick pattern as it sweeps behind the lattice pattern. Given the expense and the effort of installing a *trompe-l'oeil*, it is worth making the extra effort to get the formula right. The backdrop to the trellis should be incorporated as far as possible into the false perspective by ridding it of its own heavy and flat two-dimensional lines. Coats of thick masonry paint, or a simple render applied to the brickwork immediately within the perimeter of the *trompe*, are effective as a mask. By leaving the surrounding masonry untouched, the impact of the trellised perspective can gain from the heightened contrast.

White diamond-mesh (opposite) on walls painted terracotta pink flank an illusory archway in stone through which a fantasy view unfolds into the distance.

A longer illusion (below) derives impact from a colourful finish that shows up well both by day and, with uplights, by night.

Other props and aids can be employed: the use of a mirror or *trompe-l'oeil* painting reinforces the suggestion that the eye is being drawn through a *tonnelle* to a view beyond. A mirror will need to be angled with care to prevent the viewer from seeing him or herself. Even where the garden is small, a mirror can present a seemingly fresh scene, familiarity disguised by the unusual angle from which it is caught. A variant of this is the painting of an imaginary scene on to the focal area and surrounds of the *trompe*. Although seeming excessive in contrivance, it is no more so than the illusion engendered by the woodwork. The two can be cleverly coordinated to good effect, and the painting need not be expensive to commission.

Crucial to the success of any *trompe-l'oeil* is a thoughtful approach to the immediate setting. The foreground can be exploited, both in terms of planting (which will be dealt with in a later chapter) and ornamentation to further guide and convince the eye. If the illusion beyond is to be the main focus, the foreground should flank the view with the appropriate proportions. Alternatively, a statue or urn can be positioned centrally, perhaps on a plinth to coordinate its dimensions with the illusory opening and vanishing point of the *trompe* behind. The conclusion (and most artificial part) of the *trompe* is then subject to less clinical scrutiny, becoming a partly obscured backdrop to the stronger focus in front.

End-pieces

Fantasies and *trompe-l'oeils* are a popular feature in contemporary gardens reflecting both idle whim and also necessity, where bleak aspects threaten entire scenes. Large and hard expanses of modernity can sit heavily across a view, begging artistic relief.

Depending upon the scale of the challenge, it may be insufficient to put up the odd trellised panel, albeit nicely centred. The proportion and style of the trellis against the weight of the backdrop does require careful thought if it is to have any impact. Should diamond-mesh be used to provide contrast? Would square-mesh be too close to the wall's own pattern? How can the profile of the trellis, its colour and

planting combine? A large and rectangular piece of wall may need more than a rectangular piece of trellis-work lower down. Would a series of slim and vertical sections be better, or a diamond-mesh panel encased in a frame of square-mesh?

Very often the task can be made easier by the creation of a false horizon below the real one. With masonry paint, render, or a clinging and vigorous climber such as ivy, a different finish or texture can be applied to the walling below the new horizon, reinforcing its strength of line. The proportions of any subsequent artistry can then be presented within a smaller backdrop, the perspective of the whole scene lowered and its needs reduced. Trellised features can find effective employment in this role, elegant in detail but sufficiently architectural in their presence to provide a fitting endpiece. There is a useful parallel here in the solutions imposed on lofty interior walls where the dimensions render pictures inadequate in their impact. Architraves and rails, with changes in colour and texture, can isolate an upper section from the proportions of anything below.

Where the challenge to produce an effective treatment is considerable, one of the most pleasing approaches is in the cloistered format. In addition to trellis on a back wall, deploy arches in front, trellising between the curve of the arch, their uprights and the cross-piece that runs along the top. The cross-pieces can have finials and, if wanted, be joined to the top of the trellis on the back wall with either more trellis or a series of shorter cross-pieces. This will create a tapestry of patterns and shadows along the back of a garden or terrace. The back trellis should not be too open a mesh and, if against a wall, can even be set slightly away from the wall by means of spacing blocks to create further elements of light and shade. Thick, close-set diamond-mesh, finished in a dark colour, will suggest the garden of a Moorish courtyard and could be set behind either Gothic arches or rectangular frames with arching pelmets in fine trellis.

Another approach might be based on a galleried pergola crossing the end of the view, with an open pattern and entrance on the near side but with heavier trellis on the far side. Whatever the design, the two-stage sequence will create sufficient depth and shadow to draw the eye without revealing too much detail.

This delightful structure (opposite) set at the mid-point of a longer axis, uses its own dimensions to provide the perfect visual frame for the end-piece beyond, to which the eye is automatically drawn.

ON THE HOUSE

Roof Terraces
and Balconies

Roof terraces and balconies seek many of the same qualities as ground-level gardens, the most notable being the luxury of an outdoor 'room' and immediate extension to the house. Boundary walls, however, which serve a vital purpose in the orthodox garden, are either absent or only partially effective on a roof terrace, their design being dictated by other duties. The structural characteristics of roofs and balconies, furthermore, often preclude the easy erection of new walls. It is here that trellis-work comes into its own.

Absolutely essential to any terrace above ground level is the provision of shelter. Exposure to the natural elements is often much more intense, affecting both human and plant life. The hours of sunlight are longer and the likelihood of cooling shadows less; every breeze or gust (with or without rain) is felt more severely, and from more directions; and not only are temperatures lower in cold weather but there is less protection against them. Trellis-work can attempt to limit such extremes, using the appropriate closeness of mesh and thickness and strength of wood and plant cover.

A second function is, inevitably, the need for sufficient enclosure to secure privacy and seclusion. Complete enclosure, without any relief around eye-level, may feel claustrophobic, especially where the top of the trellis marks an abrupt division between rigid geometry below and a vast expanse of open sky above. Gardens at ground level usually have a further horizon – be it no more than the occasional tree or roof top – which is why a complete enclosure above eye-level feels like a reassuring defence rather than a restriction.

Deliberate 'windows', incorporated into the trellis, can be effective without jeopardising seclusion. They can be rounded (in a Japanese style) or involve a brief but angular break in the mesh (in a Chinese style); alternatively, an arched or pelmeted window can be employed. Instead of windows, a strategic change of pattern to a lower density of mesh (between waist and chest height) can give the impression that

Roof terraces invariably lack boundary walls and require trellising to provide a measure of shelter and seclusion. In this role, the white square-mesh surround (left) derives both strength and character from the frame of bracketed uprights fitted between firmly jointed rails, top and bottom.

With a hint of Renaissance styling (right) low diamond-mesh trellis-work, comfortably encased within sturdy uprights and cross-piece, runs across the front of a small balcony terrace outside the french windows of a drawing room. The diamond-mesh has been expanded to give the relaxed effect of flattened lozenges.

viewing is encouraged rather than prevented. Such combinations, defined and emphasized by a dado rail, can be very attractive. The more relaxed pattern above implies confidence and freedom while the finer mesh below provides shelter, privacy (especially when sitting) and a guard against anything falling from the terrace. If the terrace is likely to be used by small children, then it may be prudent to choose patterns and meshes which do not immediately suggest a climbing frame!

On balconies, the immediate need for privacy and shelter usually occurs on the wings or flanks. Where the balcony itself is narrow, the resulting trellis-work could well resemble the Japanese 'sleeve fence' (see pages 84–85), being of much greater height than width. Also appropriate (for privacy, shelter and safety) are the patterns of such 'fences', many of them incorporating both solid and latticed tiers within the same panel. The positioning and scale of trellis on a balcony, but especially across the front, must take into account its effect on the light and ambience of adjoining rooms. Trellis is also an important aid on roofs and balconies to the creation of miniature landscapes. Definition and detail may be required for the design of an area; brief internal division can produce interest; and screens can hide awkward features (which can be plentiful on exterior walls). Simple pergolas or arbours can be attractive where space and the structural capacity (of the building) allow their construction. Providing both shelter and shadows, they can be an inviting source of much-needed intimacy or mystery, elements that are not easily evoked in a starkly open setting.

Another roof-terrace and balcony role of trellis is as a means of support for vertical planting. Remember, however, that while owner and friends only venture out in good weather, the plants are there all the time. Choose plants that have a known tolerance for such conditions and consider the installation of a small irrigation system to counter the continually drying effects of wind and sun. Roof and balcony trellis must take into account both the pressure imposed on its construction and fixing by winds (especially with close meshes and liberal plant cover) and any structural implications its erection might have on a building's load-bearing or water-proofing features. If in doubt, seek qualified advice before causing what could turn out to be expensive damage or injury

to those below. In some instance, there can also be planning permission requirements. If the sideways leverage of the wind is a particular concern, lateral rails and cross-pieces (capped, dado-styled, or plinthed) can improve stability. Such additions can also be welcome from an aesthetic point of view as they provide a more imposing frame for the trellised pattern.

Walls

Expanses of walling, whatever the dimensions, can be transformed with trellis-work attached flat to their sides. The trellis not only benefits from shelter and protection,

Where entire 'walls' are fashioned from trellis-work (left) an especially pleasing effect can be achieved by using a dense mesh below waist height and a more relaxed pattern above. The latter prevents claustrophobia, the former increases safety, and the combination guards against monotony. The inclusion of a dado rail between the two patterns improves all these effects. Below left in the illustration, the trellis set around the bottom edge of the balcony acts as a fringe to the verandah at ground level.

PLANTS FOR THE ROOF TERRACE

Check suitability to local conditions, especially winter cold and associated wind chill.

Front-line Protection

Evergreen and Semi-evergreen	**Deciduous**
(Semi-evergreen refers to those plants that keep many of their leaves in milder and more protected sites.)	Berberis (some) Buddleia Caragana Chaenomeles speciosa (Flowering Quince or Japonica)
Berberis (some) Choisya ternata Cotoneaster (some) Cryptomeria japonica Elaeagnus (some) Escallonia (not for very cold sites) Euonymus fortunei radicans and cultivars Hedera (Ivy) Ilex (Holly) Juniperus Pyracantha Rhamnus Taxus (Yew) Viburnum (some)	Clematis montana Cotinus Cotoneaster (some) Diervilla lonicera Elaeagnus (some) Forsythia Hippophae Humulus lupulus (Hop) Jasminum nudiflorum Kerria japonica Kolkwitzia amabilis Philadelphus (some) Polygonum baldschuanicum (Russian Vine) Potentilla Tamarix Viburnum (some)

Additional planting where some protection is offered by immediate topography, density of trellis mesh, or other planting.

Actinidia chinesis Ceanothus (the hardier species and varieties) Clematis (the hardier species and varieties) Coronilla	Ipomoea sp. and var. (treat as an annual) Lonicera (various) Rosa (stronger climbers and ramblers) Vitis species (Vines) Wisteria

but every part of a carpented design can be secured and stable. Since it is possible to use lighter grades of timber (there being less need for load-bearing uprights and ribs) the design can be proportionately more ambitious and delicate.

Elaborate *treillage* and *trompe-l'oeils* set against walls were especially favoured in late-Victorian Britain. This use of trellis can also frequently be seen in French towns and cities, where the balance between the architecture of a building and the architectural detail of trellis is crucial to the final effect. The trellis often echoes the character of the façade behind, picking out its lines in green to contrast with the softer tones of the render.

Where the masonry has its very distinct pattern of joints and mortar, a trellised pattern superimposed on to its surface can have a confusing effect. There is insufficient contrast, for instance, between many standard square-mesh patterns and the lines of standard brickwork. The two rhythms in combination can appear repetitive and, being unsynchronized, can easily clash. Stronger contrast may be needed; if the trellis is the top priority, the walling can be rendered or painted to produce a blander background. The ultimate effect of contrast to the wall will be affected by mesh size (very dense, for instance), pattern (perhaps diamond-mesh), or finish (the choice of paints and stains).

For both practical and aesthetic reasons, trellis-work pinned to walls should not necessarily be flush to the masonry, but fractionally off-set with wall spaces, chocks or brackets; sharper and more interesting patterns of light and shadow are thus thrown on to the wall behind. The interplay of the solid trellis and its shadow adds depth and movement to what might otherwise be a static scene. If climbing plants are combined with the trellis, they also will benefit from the space and air afforded by the gap which will leave room for the development of branches and foliage.

Especially successful with diamond-mesh on walls is the use of twin layers of battens to make a framework of one or more compartments. The first layer is applied flat to the wall (to the chosen design), then the trellis is attached, and the second set of battens follows the same lines as the first, thus holding the trellis between the two sets and emphasizing the visual excitement of the diamond-mesh.

Bland areas of rendered walling can be brought to life with trellis pinned to them. The gentle curves and restraint of these panels (opposite above and below) are perfectly suited to the compact dimensions in which they are sited.

In complete contrast, this early 1900s English design (above) lacks the subtlety expressed in the city treillage of France and dominates both house and garden walls with an intensity that was then fashionable.

Alleys and Basements

Such is the pressure on space in modern urban living that views of basements and alleys can constitute the backdrop to rooms of important or regular use (especially kitchens). Such unprepossessing areas can, in their restricted dimensions, become the scene of quite intricate landscape design. Those very features that seem so uncompromisingly drab can be turned to advantage; the enclosing walls can frame a composition in which the imagination of the trellis artist can be let loose. The challenge may feel greater than in a natural setting, but the wholly architectural context of a basement or alley has significantly fewer constraints than a conventional garden (except for the physical problems of planting). Artistry and contrivance do not have to strike a careful balance with nature, a relationship that can render some efforts clumsy or pretentious. Unlike the garden, moreover, the ambience of many basements and alleys is difficult to spoil, and most such areas are improved by even the smallest intervention. Blank stretches of masonry are ideal for any sort of trellised fantasy and *trompe-l'oeils*, especially, look effective when seen through the rectangular frame of a window.

Mirrors in confined spaces not only give a convincing impression of more space, but they actually create more light. Standard trellis patterns can also be cut to frame and arch over mirrored or painted *trompes*. In such spaces as basement areas and alleys, trellis pinned flat to a wall can be exploited to the full; if it is slightly set off from the wall by means of wall spacers, the shadows so created will give the setting further visual interest.

When planning the trellis-work of an outside area, it is often worth considering whether the style, colour, texture and finish could effectively continue some of the decorative themes of the rooms overlooking the space. A gentle and soothing effect may be sought, or a more dramatic and stimulating statement could be fun. Both trellis and backdrop could, for instance, be in dark but contrasting tones (the trellis could even be black), suggestive of hidden depths and mystery. The style might be Moorish with a close-set diamond-mesh screen hinting at secret delights. It would also not require much space to site a single panel at right-angles to a wall, in the style, and perhaps pattern, of a Japanese 'sleeve fence', the recess beyond being all the more intriguing for being hidden.

If the view is along the length of a basement or alley (rather than across its width) pergola walks can be created with trellis down one or both walls and simple cross pieces above. Where there are heavy shadows from surrounding buildings, a lightness of touch will be needed overhead, unless the aim is to create a dramatic *tonnelle*, concluding either in a splash of light or deliberate darkness. A contrasting effect could be a Mediterranean one, with a vine trailing across large open-meshed trellis, terracotta tiles and white walls.

A confined area outside a drawing room window (opposite above) shows a Classical centre-piece flanked by the emphatic rhythm of rectangular trellis-work (prior to climbers). White walls, terracotta tiles and an implied arch surrounded by diamond-mesh in a honey-coloured stain (opposite below) have transformed an otherwise bleak space.

The airy nature of trellis is ideal in restricted circumstances, such as an alley by the side of a house (below), where it has been wrought into arched and pergola-ed effects.

DETAILS AND INCIDENTALS

An old-fashioned conservatory-greenhouse (right) is brightened by the pattern and finish of diamond-mesh trellis-work. Not only does it decorate a large expanse of previously blank wall, but it also encourages vertical feats of plantsmanship, an important feature for many indoor gardeners.

Verandahs, Porches and Conservatories

The potential for trellis around verandahs, porches and conservatories has usually to take into account the style of the buildings to which they are attached. The trellis is essentially in a complementary role, even where it is the only redeeming feature. There is, however, considerable precedent for its use in such circumstances. In the East, verandahs have attracted lattice designs for centuries. Traditional Islamic and Moorish designs incorporated close-set diamond-meshes beyond arched surrounds; trellised pelmets were also used between uprights. From the Orient, and China especially, came the tradition of lattice balustrading around verandahs and, overhead, lattice pelmets, more in the style of cornices. Since the nineteenth century, trellised effects on verandahs and porches have also been popular in the West. Certainly, the hard lines of many verandahs and porches can benefit from pelmets, balustrading and background detail, but the applications of trellis-work must be carried out with great sensitivity.

Conservatory trellis-work, also, is at its best when sympathetic to the mood of the main structure. Its most obvious role here is more likely to be functional than extrovert, supporting plantsmanship and internal lay-out. Not unlike the roof terrace, the vertical display of climbers and shrubs is important in conservatories and trellis-work can be vital to their impact. The area of a conservatory may also be in need of sub-division and recesses, for which trellis is ideal.

Edwardian verandahs (left) sometimes incorporated back walls covered with dazzling (but far from relaxing) treillage and trompe-l'oeil patterns. Any incongruity with the architectural façade of the house was usually ignored.

Trellis may be used to provide a specific setting for garden furniture; this seat (opposite above) is recessed between two trellised buttresses. These attractive gates (opposite below) illustrate how trellised pattern can serve the practical function of a barrier with beguiling artistry.

Gothic conservatories, especially popular today, provide a wonderful setting for trellis in *chinoiserie* or Moorish styles. Many conservatories, however, are now finished to very high standards and the trellis should look as interesting as possible, even where destined to anonymity under a rampant passion flower. There may be opportunities, furthermore, to indulge in colours and finishes not normally associated with garden trellis, especially where the conservatory is in effect an extra reception room and a continuation of the interior design of the main house.

Garden Buildings, Gates and Furniture

Various types of buildings and structures standing in a landscaped setting have traditionally attracted elaborate and strongly styled trellis-work. The lines of such buildings frequently provide the ideal framework to set off the intricate detail of trellised panels. Simple diamond-mesh, for instance, is immediately attractive when set between vertical uprights and horizontal roof edges. Porches and verandahs are often limited by being set against large blocks of masonry, but trellis-work can provide a complementary arrangement of lines and detail to soften any overall crudity of effect. Buildings in the garden, however, offer more scope, with trellis either as a substantial component or an incidental detail. Summerhouses, potting sheds, garages and lean-tos are all opportunities for artistic indulgence. Garden buildings are often functional in design as in purpose and like basements and alleys can be immensely improved in looks by the addition of trellis-work, though beware allowing the embellishment to become over-elaborate. The planting of vigorous climbers, though, can often help ease the effect of attaching trellis-work to an essentially functional building.

Garden furniture, gates and doors can also benefit from the addition of lattice designs. Their simple lines and structures are an ideal setting for pattern, and the pattern, in turn, complements the more substantial frame.

The impact of using trellis in such roles is enhanced by the conspicuously practical nature of the structure in question. Gates

and doors, for instance, employ trellis less as a random detail and more as the means for a continuing view. Garden furniture can also indulge in mild illusions of comfort, the trellised pattern suggesting a sprung effect.

Furniture styles have resisted changes in fashion elsewhere in the garden, remaining popular in every form, from Rococo and *trompe-l'oeil* to Moorish patterns in white marble and endless versions of Chinese Chippendale. Rustic patterns and Gothic details have also survived centuries of change, still incorporating lattice in one form or another.

As a detail of more miscellaneous features, trellis has constantly been called upon to display its versatility. The flower basket edgings of the French *corbeille* and some of Repton's schemes are now rare, but other fashions have taken their place. One example follows the principle of a string vest: ingenious and attractive trellis-work in the style of sentry boxes and minute *pavillons de treillage* are employed by some to protect plants against winter cold. These are mobile structures that come out of storage just as the garden furniture needs to be put away for winter.

CONSTRUCTION, INSTALLATION AND MAINTENANCE

Well-constructed and maintained trellis is ideally suited to the transformation of today's compact garden. Here, the garden entrance via a side alley has been imaginatively handled with crisp square-mesh trellising generously off-set from the walls. The stylish addition of capping rails strengthens the trellis and makes it a more effective support for the climbers.

FORM IN TRELLIS

This graceful and elegant design (below) is superbly restrained in its detail, but derives considerable charm from the subtle contrast between two different square-meshes, a rectangular-mesh and the optical illusion of the dome. In a garden setting, either as an end-piece or to provide internal division, such varied form is an effective way of transforming the most unpromising space.

Since the first enclosures of land around his dwelling, man has taken pride in organizing his immediate surroundings and using them for his own ends. Within the garden, trellis is an obvious assertion of our confident presence and unashamed manipulation of the landscape. Its architectural form, combining symmetry and orderly pattern, is a way of exercising control over a potentially unruly environment. Whether used as a purely horticultural device for supporting vines, a method of design for creating enclosure, an unseen means for shaping planting or as an architectural end in itself, its form and pattern have reflected our view of garden design.

Despite the current fashion for 'wild' areas in garden design and our concern with ecological issues, the modern garden has many similar characteristics of those of the Italian Renaissance, its layout being motivated by composition, interest, convenience and enjoyment. Where gardens are immediately adjacent to the house, confined in dimension, and set among surroundings which are patently beyond the control of the gardener, they develop as natural extensions of the home, becoming subject to intense and varied use. In this context, trellis-work has come to be regarded as a highly versatile medium, providing and combining both necessary means and delightful ends. The garden as 'outdoor room' is expected to provide more: it also has to serve as a reception area, with all that it implies in terms of finish and comfort. Trellis can bring elegance to a garden in a flowing and rhythmic architectural form, and still serve a practical purpose. It is an especially obvious component in the garden which is compact in either dimension or usage. Its use in the larger landscape, however, has been much more subject to fashion and style – monumental in eighteenth-century France and late nineteenth-century Britain, but ignored by the English landscape school as being too strong an intervention by man in the 'natural' world.

This gazebo (right above) is a cheerful compilation of rounded and Gothic arches, diamond-mesh and the tiers of ascending ribs that comprise the roof's precise pattern

The exciting form of this roof-terrace trellis (right centre) was dictated by the need to provide access to the view beyond while providing a safety barrier for small children.

The need to block the view of a neighbour's carport led to an exciting architectural solution in trellis – the surmounting of an existing fence with a series of Gothic arches (right below).

PATTERN IN TRELLIS

Square-mesh

The square-mesh of the earliest forms of trellis was both simple in design and logical in purpose, encouraging the main stems of vines upwards and their laterals outwards. A square grid of true verticals and true horizontals has also sometimes been read as symbolic of predestined order and 'natural' symmetry.

Square-mesh is a pattern that tends to rigid definition rather than easy flow. Each vertical delineates the exact height of the panel or structure, and each horizontal does likewise across the width. You can either look up the trellis or along it, and to that extent (unless the mesh is interwoven), there will be some movement, its direction depending on which way round the panel is installed. With vertical struts proud, there is less lateral momentum, the eye tending to be slowed by the repetitive upward movement of the lines; any view that is unfolding will therefore feel longer. With the horizontals proud, the eye is subject to a greater forwards pull.

Different grades and sizes of square-mesh can convey different moods. With their disinclination to flow some have a certain heavy quality about them and need enlivening with some embellishment. Denser meshes have more character but not necessarily any more movement. A novel variation are the tram-line patterns (as used in some Japanese trellises) which many would associate with the 'set' of a Scottish tartan. Another very attractive variation is rectangular mesh, with the longer sides on the vertical axis.

A very large and open structured square-mesh, in a sturdy grade of wood, has a heavy, plodding feel that lacks charm when set against or arranged along the top of walls. Open patterns, however, come into their own when used across the tops of pergolas, allowing plenty of light to filter down.

When installing square-mesh trellis, it is important to choose the most suitable face. With horizontal struts proud (opposite above left), there is a strong lateral pull on the eye; while with verticals proud (opposite above right), the eye is drawn upwards rather than along. Where square-mesh flanks a receding view, dominant vertical struts seem to make its unfolding more leisurely, since they slow the forward movement of the eye.

This plan for an end-piece derives proportion and style from both its outline and contrasting mesh sizes. Set along the top of a wall, it would express a strong upward and onward feel from its uprights, finials and dominant vertical struts. This upward momentum is only partly tempered by the horizontal mood of brickwork below. A more restful effect would be achieved by making the horizontal struts dominant in al the panels or even just in the larger and more prominent mesh of the three taller panels.

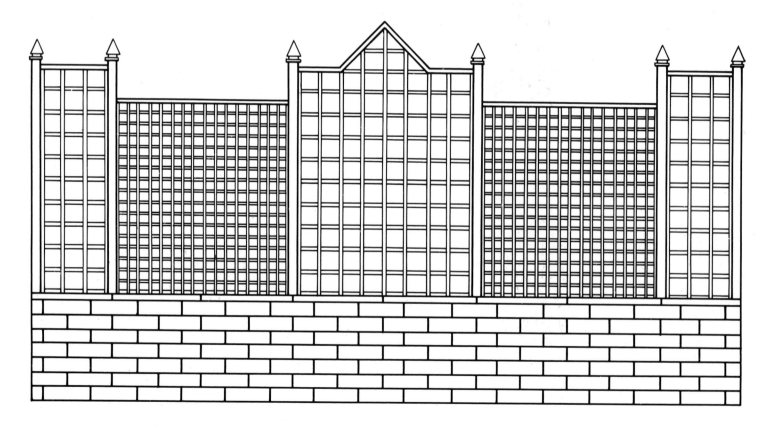

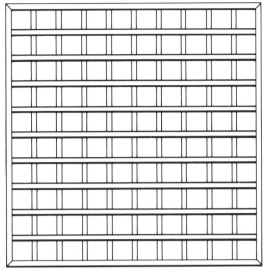

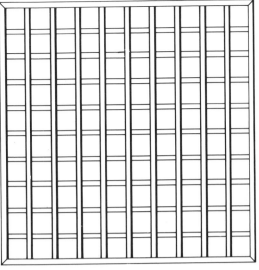

This white square-mesh on a roof terrace (below) is secured by a plinth rail, sturdy and frequent uprights, and (out of picture) a capping rail with finials. The mesh is slightly smaller than the standard to give a measure of shelter and privacy. Ivies and other climbers, all from pots and troughs, are just beginning to establish some cover.

The inherently static character of square-mesh can be very welcome where a feeling of tranquillity is sought. Its solid predictability can be a source of comfort and relief. It can also be strategically used when contrasted with busier or more dramatic areas of trellis nearby.

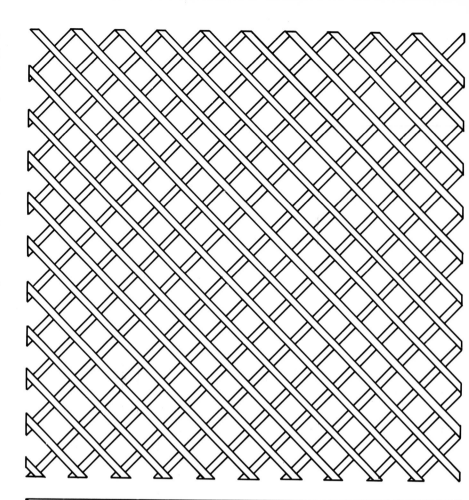

Diamond-mesh

The appearance of diamond-mesh patterns makes a marked contrast to square-mesh. Diamond-mesh flows with a more graceful and airy ease to achieve its effects. Much of this flow comes from the fact that its lines run diagonally away from the vertical and horizontal, tending to disguise the exact dimensions of the space it is covering, and leading the eye to the broad effect rather than on a distinct axis.

In its cheerful contrast to the profile of many other structures, diamond-mesh often seems to imply a deliberate attempt at artistry and imagination, making it a useful design component in landscapes in built-up areas, where there is a relentless preponderance of heavy vertical and horizontal lines. It can be refreshing in both character and form, an important attribute where it is important that garden trellis is not too suggestive in its line of surrounding walls and buildings. Thus, the diamond pattern can combine well with unrendered brickwork. In Persian gardens, the diagonal mesh was developed in heavier trellis, providing screens for privacy, seclusion and shade. Close-set diamond-mesh has continued as a feature of Islamic and Moorish design, and to Western eyes can still conjure up Eastern mystery.

In the West, the Renaissance garden maintained the Roman habit of creating garden compartments with low diamond-mesh trellis fences, but paid much more attention to the ribs and uprights that accompanied such structures. The combination of diagonal flow within a strong frame is one of the most appealing combinations in traditional trellis-work and is often used in garden structures and garden furniture as well as panels.

Without the frame, the visual impact of diamond-mesh can suffer from having indistinct and seemingly unfinished edges. It is preferable, then, to add a frame, both for

The diagonals cross at right-angles to produce a relaxed and balanced pattern of perfect diagonally-set squares in this plan for diamond-mesh trellis (opposite above). Without a frame, however, diamond-mesh can seem visually and structurally inconclusive. The lower panel (opposite below), has more character and movement with its sharper pattern of vertical lozenges; the solidity of the perimeter completes the picture and lends the panel strength.

Flanked by lilies, an uncompromisingly bright and lively combination (right), is this white diamond-mesh set against a yellow wall. In complete contrast (below) the dark shadows behind this 'Repton blue' trellis give exact definition to the smaller mesh, heavier grade of timber and carpented detail.

sturdiness and visual effect. This becomes an absolute necessity in the case of the mass-produced 'expanding' diamond-mesh which is invariably flimsy and short-lived unless set against a wall. Expansion or contraction of panels of diamond-mesh on site does have the advantage of offering a choice of pattern. Opened to the specified dimensions, the detail of the mesh should form perfect squares, though on a diagonal axis. Opened to a lesser or greater degree, it can make a sharp (and possibly busy) pattern of thin lozenges which might be appropriate for a Gothic scene. Diamond-mesh, incidentally, is not so easily used as a climbing frame. This has a security implication which will be considered later.

Combinations

Combinations of different trellis meshes and patterns should be approached with care. They carry immense potential for elegance, as has been seen in some of the *treillage* of the last four centuries. They are also superb where trellis-work is destined to be a comparatively large feature of a single scene. On a roof terrace, for instance, it may be the only element that can provide enclosure, running from ground level to six feet or more in height. The same repetitive pattern throughout could become an oppressively boring expanse, so contrasting proportions and patterns may be used to transform what might otherwise have been bleak repetition into a delightful enclosure.

Combinations that are ill-planned or hopelessly extravagant can be visually unsettling. At the turn of the last century, the rage for *treillage* was often inspired more by ostentation than sense with ambitious amalgamations of pattern, both indoors and out, lost under a welter of competing intricacy. From the Strathpeffer Spa in Scotland to shops in Bond Street, endless meshes and *trompe-l'oeils* created overpowering and disturbing surroundings, without the relief afforded by surrounding planting.

Understanding the very different moods evoked by square-mesh and diamond-mesh trellis is essential to successfully combining the two. One of the best formats is where square-mesh is placed as a frame around a larger area of diamond-mesh. The former is restful and solid in effect, its natural restraint flattering the movement inherent in the latter. Even finer was the combination proposed by Henry Holland for the Prince Regent at Carlton House. There, diamond-mesh was framed within a frame of circular mesh. To achieve the effect of a static centre and a flowing rim, encase a square-mesh panel with a diamond-mesh frame.

Another important use for combinations is in a sequence of structures which offer contrast in pattern and profile, but in effect create a single visual entity. Cloisters are an example where trellis arches and associated detail can be set forward of further detailing behind. For example, the lively qualities of diamond-mesh can be brought out around the arches, with the backdrop (in the shadows) relaxing into the finality of square-mesh. Alternatively, the opposite

combination can work, especially in very small areas, where the backdrop is not required to look too static. Diamond-mesh panels set in the shadow of Gothic arches are an exciting sight.

Combining square or diamond-meshes with Oriental patterns requires care. Certainly *chinoiserie* panels have been successfully incorporated into larger designs, especially where their open character is framed by a much denser square-mesh. True Chinese styles would not make happy components of a *treillage* scheme.

It is to the East, however, that one looks for the ultimate expression of imaginative combination. Tiered across the same panel, the Japanese explore variations of detail, pattern, density and substance to a degree that has no comparison in the West.

The enthusiasm for treillage early this century led to complex combinations of meshes both indoors and out, as in this very Edwardian scheme (right) at Strathpeffer Spa, Scotland.

The two wall-panel designs (below) illustrate contrasting combinations of square- and diamond-mesh. The 'doorway' of diamond-mesh (right) hints at further views unfolding beyond a surround of fixed and solid masonry. In contrast, the diamond-mesh surround (left), suggests a tented entrance, a lively prelude to static repose beyond.

STYLE

Classical and Gothic

Transforming the wider landscape or architectural backdrop may be impossible, but not so one's own garden, which can be indulged with a style that reflects circumstance and personal taste. Whatever the result, most people would wish to see it as being in keeping with the setting. But this should not mean that it excludes deliberate melodrama, incongruity and surprise. Where the setting is dreary, monotonous or constricted, a sharp infusion of creative trellis-work may be exactly what is required. The trellised obelisks of the seventeenth-century Netherlands served such a purpose. The disappointing backgrounds to many contemporary gardens, roof terraces

and basements can be a blessing in disguise for artistry, requiring less conformity, allowing wider choice and begging greater inspiration.

Classical styles induce feelings of order and familiarity, using proportions which have been hugely popular and widely imitated over the centuries. Strong vertical uprights, kept in check by reassuring right-angles, horizontal cornices and firm roof lines, create very satisfying frames for the rhythmic patterns of trellis; and the ease with which a Palladian profile can create a series of balanced compartments has made it an ideal vehicle for *treillage*. Unless the detail, embellishment or overall dimensions are startling, the Classical style is solid and settling in effect and rarely controversial.

Detractors of the Classical would accuse it of smug predictability; and, indeed, where trellised details fail to add the required zest, contrast may be needed in the surrounding planting and layout. Gothic styles and idioms are very often more immediately exciting in character. Sharper edges, incised embellishment, tapering finials, and busy roof lines suggest a more extrovert approach to garden design. Gothic styles suggest much more movement than the Palladian and a greater potential for exoticism and mystery. Combined with trellis the effect tends to instant drama, but care does need to be exercised in keeping elaboration within check.

The Classical proportions of this end-piece plan (opposite) are emphasized by the simple vertical lines held easily in check under the strong horizontal lines of roofs and cornices, yet this design remains very relaxed despite using a combination of different meshes and a measure of implied perspective to suggest an arched colonnade.

The ease with which Classical and Palladian styles could be expressed in treillage encouraged designers in eighteenth-century France and late-Victorian Britain to indulge in ever more fanciful pattern, detail and architectural effect, as in this plan for an enclosed garden (below). In this type of ambitious design, the opportunity for false perspectives and elaborate embellishment was often exploited.

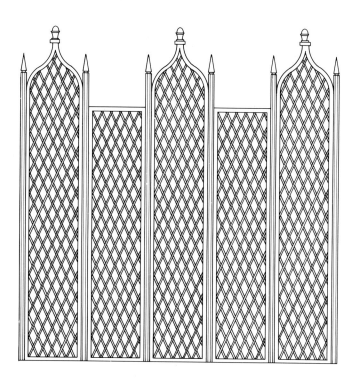

The Gothic atmosphere in this trellis plan (left), is created by slim, arching panels held by uprights that are fluted and chamfered below tapering finials. The effect from both trellis and surround is of sharp upward lines, dramatic detail and constant movement.

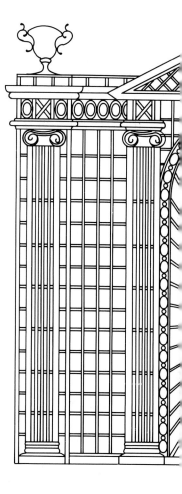

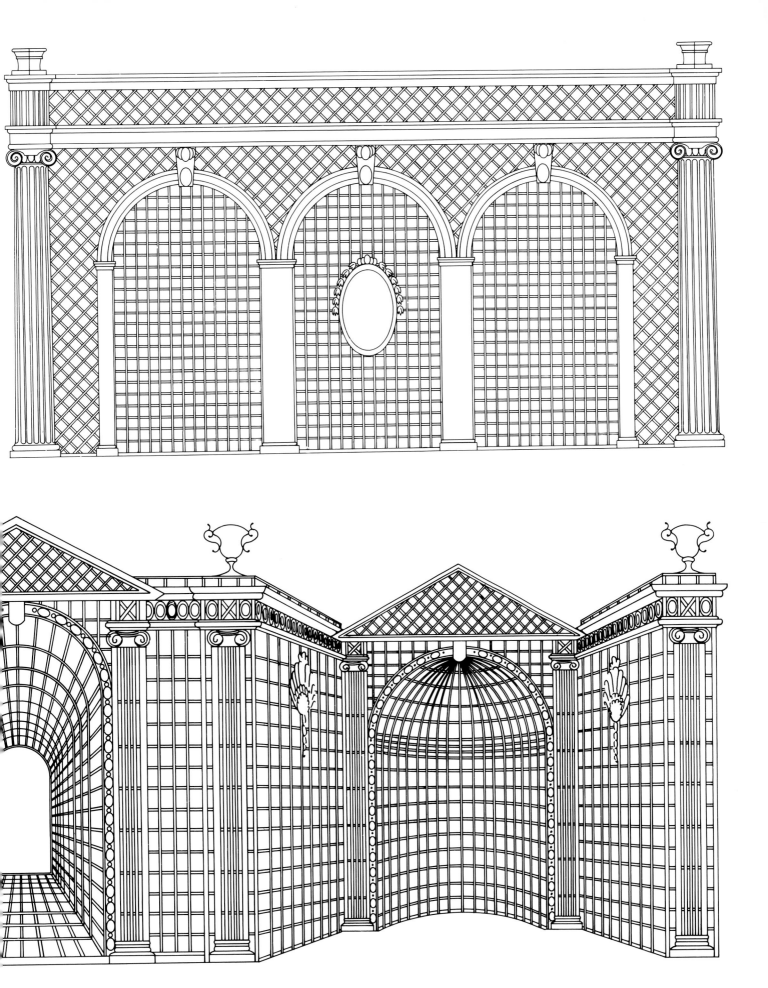

Chinese

In the East, an essential characteristic of any garden is that the visitor, as he progresses through the garden, should be presented with a series of unfolding themes and views. Internal division is therefore fundamental to garden design and, as in the West, relies notably on the versatility of lattice work, manipulating the way things are seen, with frames that focus the attention, screens that hide and patterns that deliberately give no more than an incomplete glimpse of what lies beyond.

In the Chinese garden, invariably, the visitor's progress through the garden is further controlled by a gallery, arcade or *lang*. This would snake through the garden on a carefully planned course from house verandah to garden pavilions and pagodas, leading the visitor via a progression of scenes. Many of these structures include trellis balustrades, pelmets, shutters and (in the case of pagodas) roofs, their design and embellishment immaculately wrought in either a natural finish or bolder colour.

To the Western eye, the array of lattice patterns is astonishing, illustrating the flexibility of the trellised medium in the hands of the Chinese designers. Balance and overall symmetry are rarely missing, however, even in seemingly random designs, such as 'cracking ice', which initially looks like a lattice equivalent of crazy paving or fractured glass (a pierced effect that was also used in Islamic screens).

Because of the symbolism and intricacy of their conception, Chinese lattice patterns are rarely obscured by planting; unlike much Western trellis, which can appear clumsy and crude if not partly covered by planting, Chinese trellis adds meaning to a garden design through its subtle and evocative qualities. In Chinese design, the garden is a part of man, and man is a part of nature.

Trellis-work, however, was only rarely an ingredient of the main boundary wall of the traditional Chinese garden, but it was used in standard mesh where climbers, vegetables, and cutting flowers need support. In this role, an interesting variation has been the use of twin rows of trellis in which the planting is enclosed. The trellis

The lattice-work of the 'House of Confucius', from Sir William Chambers' Views of the Gardens and Buildings at Kew (1763) (below) was a more authentic attempt at the Chinese style than many other examples of the recurrent vogue for chinoiserie in the Western world.

This trellised pavilion in Old Westbury Gardens, Long Island, draws inspiration from China both in styling and in basic garden design (right). The Chinese believed a visitor should be guided through the landscape via galleried and latticed walkways.

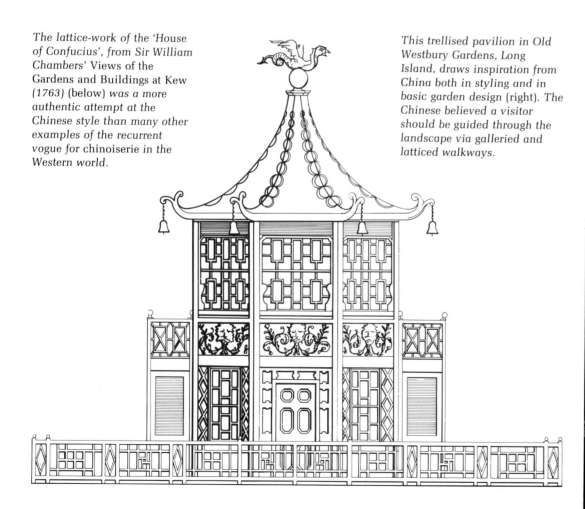

A typically Japanese-inspired composition (right) is simple in its combination of different elements. The water unites and reflects a perfectly proportioned lattice-work bridge, the graceful lines of a weeping tree and contrasting areas of light and shadow.

The Japanese 'sleeve fence' (below) invariably employed varying textures and patterns in horizontal tiers up its tall but slim dimensions. Used as screens to hide or guide, the design of the fences represents a much more subtle approach to combinations of pattern than the treillage of Europe and America.

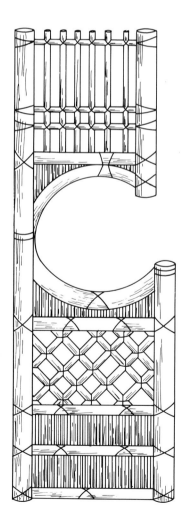

would be set about a foot apart on either side of the planting, rising to about three feet in height, then topped with a flat trellis roof. Trellis, especially when close meshed, can thus provide considerable protection.

Japanese

From China's Tang dynasty (618–907) onwards, Japanese gardens were influenced by Chinese design and practice. The Japanese garden has, however, retained its distinctiveness, largely through the application of the principles of Shintoism to its design; these express a reverence for nature and an acute sense of scale and proportion.

Internal division and the arrangement of succeeding views are achieved with screens or 'sleeve fences'. These 'fences' usually use at least one internal tier of lattice and tend to be on the opposite axis to the internal fence in Europe, being two or three times higher than they are wide (fences two feet wide and six feet high being quite common). Their elaborate patterns and designs are delightful, offering a wide choice of effect and symbolism, each termed accordingly with titles such as 'tea whisk and lattice', or 'leaning plum tree'. Rather than the abbreviations, angular deviations and lineal flow of the Chinese motif, Japanese lattice screens exploit pattern for contrasts of style, density and texture, with arrangements in horizontal tiers within the same panel. These can include standard mesh designs, but they are wrought from bamboo which imparts a livelier and more natural feel than carpented wood, while still remaining more elegant in composition than the Rustic designs of the West. The use of bamboo is encouraged by Shinto traditions, be it cut, split or directly trained from growing plants, their stems woven as trellis-work with foliage sprouting along the pattern of the mesh.

Shinto principles also encourage the use of native plant material, from bracken fibres to the tendrils of such climbers as wisteria, clematis and vine, for securing the lattice joints and other details. Some adornment, however, is not precluded and, in place of tendrils, dyed cords have sometimes been used. Circular windows, frames (the circular frame being seen as an exquisite prelude to a view) and other rounded patterns are also common within or around Japanese lattice screens (prompting such terms for the patterns as 'round window clothes horse' and 'moon entering'). Through such apertures can be trained, with patience, the trunks of trees and climbers. The association of screen and nearby planting is of great importance, both visually and symbolically; but, as in Chinese design, the detail of the lattice itself is rarely obscured. 'Sleeve fences' have one obvious application in the Western garden – as screens on the wings of balconies.

Rustic, Contemporary and Functional

In contrast to the Orient, the Western design tradition has used pattern, style and proportion in a very broad sense. The smaller details have only been important as compo-

nents of the larger effect, and have thus tended to repetition. The search for fresh idioms in the West has, however, produced renewed enthusiasm for Oriental styles. They promise a more relaxed and introspective feel, their gentler yet endlessly ingenious patterns expressed in a less overt symmetry but nonetheless suggesting a deep sense of balance. This mood of intrigue and mystery has tempted some very successful combinations of Oriental and Gothic. The fusion is enhanced where the sharper features of the Gothic profile frame, and contrast with, the softer rhythms of Chinese panels.

Gothic motifs and decoration have also been regularly used as an embellishment to Rustic styles of trellis-work. Such additional detail can redeem and transform what might otherwise feel unfinished or contrived. Trellis is, in concept, purely architectural and thus does not always lend

A bold and provocative design (right) pulls the eye to the view beyond with its wide-set diamond-mesh panels. The flattened arches and fluted columns provide a frame for both view and panels while their unexpected proportions are emphatically contemporary.

A beautifully proportioned bridge at Pusey House, Oxfordshire (opposite), combines the gentle rhythm of chinoiserie panels with the piquant finish of Gothic finials, demonstrating the architectural flexibility of trellis.

itself to noticeably haphazard design. It does suit the relaxed and quaint understatement, however, and the Rustic use of unsawn timber and natural effects is very effective when lifted by just a hint of artistry.

Rustic styles are often very appropriate to arches over garden paths, especially when these are accompanied by relatively unruly climbers. In the vegetable garden and herbaceous border, simple Rustic structures may be needed for clematis, rose, honeysuckle and sweet peas. Looser joints, more rounded timbers, rougher textures and an ad hoc air can sometimes be more fitting than the abrupt lines and white paint of an immaculate obelisk. The closer Rustic structures get to the regimented lines of buildings or formal garden design, however, the more susceptible they will be to accusations of quaint pretension and the greater their need to be partly hidden by vigorous climbers.

The apparent preponderance of trellis that is bland, predictable and functional is not unique to today's landscape and it would be a mistake for the historical perspective to suggest otherwise. Over thousands of years, communities have enclosed and sub-divided their gardens and engaged in numerous pursuits there within simple wooden structures. A noticeably contemporary feature, however, is that garden fashion is as important in the small garden as it is in the larger landscape. There is, thus, considerable incentive to indulge functionally designed trellis-work with cheerful embellishment. Stains and paints can lift blandness and, although easiest applied before installation, fresh coats and different tones can be added later.

Posts can be topped with plinth-like caps, chamfered or fluted, or carpented with such effects as 'fishtails'. These might indeed act as plinths for finials, varying from round balls to tapering Gothic plumes. Setting a second plinth, recessed in from the first, will enhance the artistry and reduce the dimensions required of the finial above. Balancing the proportions of finial, plinth and structure is important. Carpented finials can be expensive if they have to be specially commissioned. There are other options, however, from outlets for rounded wooden knobs (for furniture) and the carved additions required for banisters, balustrading and curtain poles. There are also a number of less orthodox but affordable substitutes. The balls of ball-cocks, painted appropriately, can produce large and effective spherical finials.

Turning to the trellised pattern itself, make sure that square-meshes are erected with the best bias (i.e. either verticals or horizontals proud) for the setting. Capping rails running slightly proud along the tops of panels (and possibly moulded to give a gently peaked effect) are an easy and quick addition that immediately give the pattern they frame a more flattering context. Bottom rails, also proud (in the style of a plinth), will do likewise.

More dramatic is the addition of a dado rail across a body of mesh, breaking the pattern into two sections, lending internal interest and giving the effect of a series of smaller panels. More than one dado rail can be used if the composition needs to be further subdivided.

Simple trellising can gain considerable character from the addition of appropriate rails and uprights, as this model for a post demonstrates (below left); it gains elegance and interest from the rounded finial, while the section bolted to the wall is finished off with a 'fishtail'. The short 'shoulder' panel (below) effectively negotiates changing ground levels and the resulting profile is all the more impressive for the strong capping rail and finials.

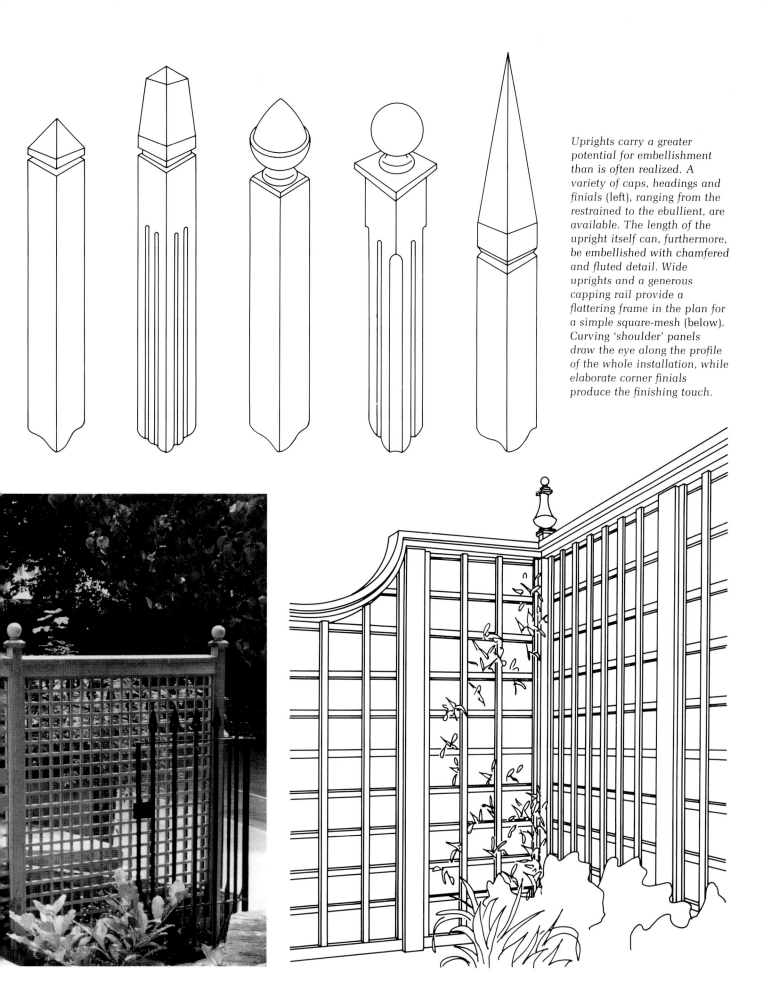

Uprights carry a greater potential for embellishment than is often realized. A variety of caps, headings and finials (left), ranging from the restrained to the ebullient, are available. The length of the upright itself can, furthermore, be embellished with chamfered and fluted detail. Wide uprights and a generous capping rail provide a flattering frame in the plan for a simple square-mesh (below). Curving 'shoulder' panels draw the eye along the profile of the whole installation, while elaborate corner finials produce the finishing touch.

COLOUR

A masterful interior (opposite) is enlivened with both exotic planting and green diamond-mesh trellising which makes a strongly architectural effect against the background.

A subtle combination of pale yellow, blue and grey (below right) gives a unique and refreshing flavour to this Thwaites and Pitt design. More startling (below), though in keeping with Oriental precedent, a relaxed lattice pattern is given a vibrant red finish.

European tradition has permanently dabbled in bright colours, either as gilded detail or, more bravely, as a response to Oriental fashion (a supreme example being Chambers' red lacquer pagoda at Kew). Trellis in Renaissance gardens included greens, blue-greens and reds. In the main, however, green, white and natural finishes have predominated in more recent times and green, especially, has been explored in all its different tones. Popular in France has been 'Monet green', which is softer than the Renaissance greens or the 'bottle' greens which are in vogue at present. Its watery hue does not always produce sufficient contrast to flatter the softer tones of some climbers, each diluting rather than setting off the other. Where the trellis is for artistic effect alone, this is not a problem. Similarly challenging and attractive is 'Repton blue'.

Both trellis and backdrop can contribute to an overall colour scheme. The vision of the garden as an outdoor 'room' has encouraged fresh ideas. White diamond-mesh over creamy lemon walls has the sharp and busy flavour of a conservatory or sun room, the colour best kept in check by the lattice being in a thick grade of wood and/or a different finish. A more subdued yellow with deep, almost brown, under-tones (brown paint stains can be mixed into the pot of yellow on site) behind rectangular trellis in a deep wood stain is a more tranquil combination, suggesting the warmth and tones associated with Mediterranean pergolas. All sorts of effects can be wrought, and nowhere is there such latitude as on balcony and roof terraces, which very obviously act as extensions to indoor rooms.

As a general rule, startling finishes (including white) are better employed in more architectural settings, while subdued finishes suit a more natural atmosphere. There may still be a need to provide emphasis, drama, surprise or an outlet for personal taste, so exceptions are valid. White finishes should be used with great caution on both trellis and backdrop. White tends to give stark emphasis, especially in an otherwise non-white environment. Thus, a garden that needs to be made to look larger than it really is, or a trellis composition which should be quite discreet either because of design or function should avoid it. White also loses its lustre and appeal more than most other colours and treatments when it weathers.

MATERIALS

Wood

The extensive use of trellis-work in today's often compact landscapes calls for close attention to the quality of materials employed in its construction. The fixtures and fittings of a garden are too often viewed as requiring a lower standard of specification than is the case within the home. Yet many gardens are, in effect, a continuation of the house, providing an extra living room. Thus, while specifications may often be lower, expectations are not, and considerable disappointment and annoyance results from premature obsolescence. Material, construction, preservation, installation and maintenance are all essential ingredients of the formula. Success should enable the practical and aesthetic benefits of trellis to be long-lasting in both pleasure and value-for-money. Short cuts and omissions will too often lead to ultimate disappointment, with trellis disintegrating just as associated planting, and the rest of the setting, are approaching maturity.

Wood remains much the most common material employed for trellising. In its different forms, however, there has always been considerable variation in price, availability, ease of carpentry, visual impact, strength and longevity. The evolution of trellis-work illustrates this breadth, from the simple to the intricate. While split bamboo trellis has always been popular in Japan, the West indulged initially in poles of unsawn hazel and willow. As carpentry improved, these and other woods (such as juniper and larch) were used sawn or unsawn, according to need. The Natural and Rustic styles of the nineteenth-century, for instance, employed unsawn timber, gnarled and knotted yew and the bran-

ched configuration of apple and pear wood. As the demand for artistry developed, sweet chestnut lattice and oak frames were frequently specified (especially on the Continent), oak being generally admired for its longevity, carpented texture and pale tones. The more elaborate structures of eighteenth-century France went further, including such refinements as ebony rims. Of undoubted suitability to all garden structures has been elm, its strength and longevity remarkable, even in water. Dutch elm disease has sadly reduced its availability.

The twentieth century may not be remembered for its innovative styles of trellis, but it has seen significant change in the types of wood used. There has been a huge growth in the use of carpented softwoods in the landscape, their usefulness improved by technical innovation. More recently, environmental concern for the future of hardwood forests has given further encouragement to the use of softwoods. Their pre-treatment is vital both if their life-span is to be maximized and their maintenance minimized. Such, however, is the quality of today's better pre-treatments and preservatives that there is now less reason to insist on hardwoods simply for longevity.

While hardwoods are less often demanded or needed, there are situations for which they remain a sensible choice. If, in addition to the expected rigours of time and weather, there has to be an additional resistance to rough physical use or battering, then the inherent resilience of hardwoods promises a longer-lasting product. There are also instances where timber is load-bearing but, for various reasons (usually decorative), has to be limited to dimensions that preclude the safe use of softwoods. Corner braces, for instance, between the uprights and cross-pieces of a heavy-topped pergola, arbour or gazebo have to bear considerable strain. While the rest of the structure can be in softwood, the load-bearing function of the brace will be best served by hardwoods. Trellis panels are sometimes essential to the stability of a larger structure and they also can derive the necessary strength from a strategic component (such as a frame) being carpented in hardwood. If, in both instances, the difference between the woods is noticeable to the eye, it will need to be masked with climbers, paint or a strong stain.

There are also purely visual motives for preferring hardwood carpentry. A much

The crisp detail of both the chinoiserie panels and the Moorish structure of this charming pavilion plan (below) would lose some of its clarity if carpented in soft-wood. Similarly, any load-bearing parts could benefit from being in hardwood.

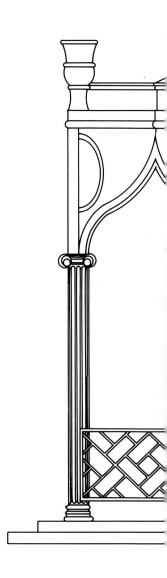

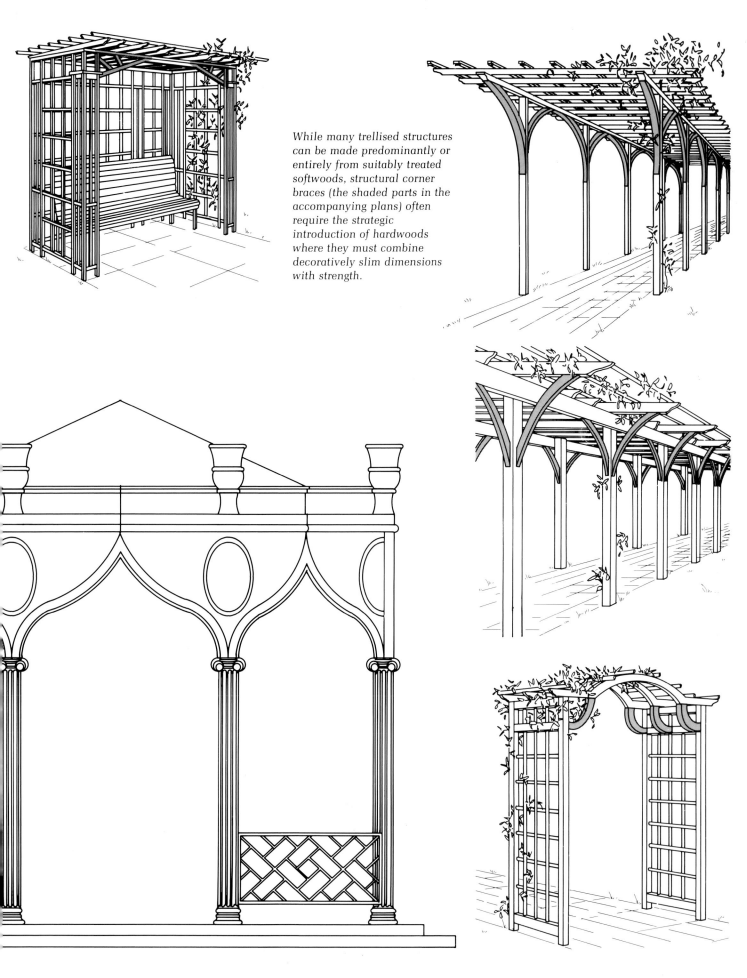

While many trellised structures can be made predominantly or entirely from suitably treated softwoods, structural corner braces (the shaded parts in the accompanying plans) often require the strategic introduction of hardwoods where they must combine decoratively slim dimensions with strength.

more precise finish and finer texture and detail can be achieved than is possible with softwoods. Of the hardwoods, iroko is one of the more readily available but, whatever the choice, care should be taken where possible as to whether its source is properly managed and regenerating.

The basic quality of the timber used for trellis is important, however effective modern preservatives may be and however skilfully its installation is carried out. It will be subject to stress from the initial preparation and carpentry; there is further strain during fixing; and continuing pressures from weather and planting ensue. Poor timber, be it from knotting or having been reduced to dimensions for which it has little inherent strength, is too readily used for commercial reasons; but it suffers accordingly. Where conditions or expectations are demanding, thicker grades and a good quality of timber will prove a wise investment.

Metals and Plastic

While medieval gardens sometimes used iron uprights to support wooden trellis-work, it was in Renaissance Italy that it was first wrought into latticed patterns. The fashion spread northwards in the three following centuries through the inspiration and artistry of craftsmen such as Tijou, Bakewell and Papworth. Iron lattice was a frequent ingredient of railings and balustrading, predominantly black in colour, but often with its detail picked out in gold and other bright hues. Some, including Bakewell, experimented with large expanses of colour. Trellis-work in wrought iron, however, remained both comparatively expensive and a logistical challenge where there was some distance between craftsman and consumer.

The advent of cast iron techniques and railways in the nineteenth century gave a boost to all forms of iron work. It was heavier and more brittle than wrought iron, and demanded meticulous protection from rust; but with its moulds, it was particularly suited to designs that relied on flowing pattern rather than intricate detail. Trellis was an obvious candidate for manufacture in this way. The present century has seen the use of metals evolve further, galvanized mild steels and aluminium being less cumbersome and brittle but offering the same

In this modern American recreation of an Italian garden wire trellis-work is set off from the wall to provide a delicate emphasis to the arched recesses behind. Wire can express intricate detail with the lightest touch; here, rhythm and vitality appear to flow across the lozenge-patterned mesh through the minute undulations in the wire.

Reminiscent in shape of those seventeenth- and eighteenth-century arbours in the style of arched sentry boxes, Geoffrey Jellicoe designed this metal trellis (opposite right) at Sutton Place in Surrey to bring a graceful precision to this jasmine-clad retreat. The impression of elegant clarity in the structure would probably have been harder to achieve in timber.

The abstract writing of this contemporary arbour illustrates a freedom of expression in trellis-work that is more readily achievable in iron and steel than in timber.

Metals can be wrought and cast to create flowing, open effects with a delightful economy of material. This elegant iron canopy (opposite) floats airily upwards from the uncompromising gravity of the stone pillars below.

potential for artistry. As trellis-work, their main use has been in garden furniture.

A nineteenth-century by-product of the booming market for cast iron was wire, a material that has been present as trellis-work ever since. The Victorian era saw the fashion at its most ambitious but the *treillage* that resulted is not sought to any great extent except in the occasional reproduction of mid-nineteenth-century arbours and gazebos. More often, wire trellising is as lacking in style as the very plain Victorian rose arch. Its market is widespread, however, since such trellis is cheap and functional, lightweight and tough, and easy in both transport and installation.

Plastic trellising has the same lightweight flexibility as wire and may seem to promise greater longevity than wood. However, such promise may well be unrealized, especially if there is any stress around the joints. There are also trel-

lised gazebos available in durable glass-fibre.

Trellis can also be fashioned from living plants. The Japanese have achieved exquisite results with bamboos, the foliage that is encouraged along the interlocking stems giving the effect of frilled lattice. In America, shrubs and trees have been pleached into free-standing trellis patterns (or 'Belgian fencing'). With refreshing imagination and a little help from wire-work, flat walls have also been decorated with climbers that are trained similarly (ivy proving suitable because of the ruthless manner in which it can be pruned and led). There are obvious instances when such 'trellis' is successful, the pattern enhanced by the natural qualities of the plant in question, be they flowers, fruit or autumn foliage. More orthodox, though no longer in vogue, is for low evergreens to be clipped into the lattice pattern of a knot garden.

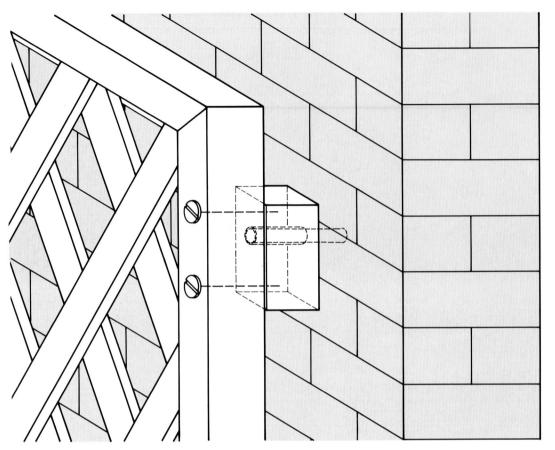

Trellis-work erected flat to a wall enjoys numerous benefits when marginally off-set with chocks (left), old cotton reels or metal brackets. Air can then circulate between the trellis and the wall to reduce the build-up of permanent damp that will both weaken the woodwork and travel through the masonry into the house; the space also provides a healthier and easier environment for climbers.

Well-constructed trellis can explore every type of geometry. Gentle rectangles, set vertically, have a gracious and elegant air; sharp rectangles, of much greater length than width, can appear Oriental on either axis; and 'tram-lines' (below) can have a very light-hearted look.

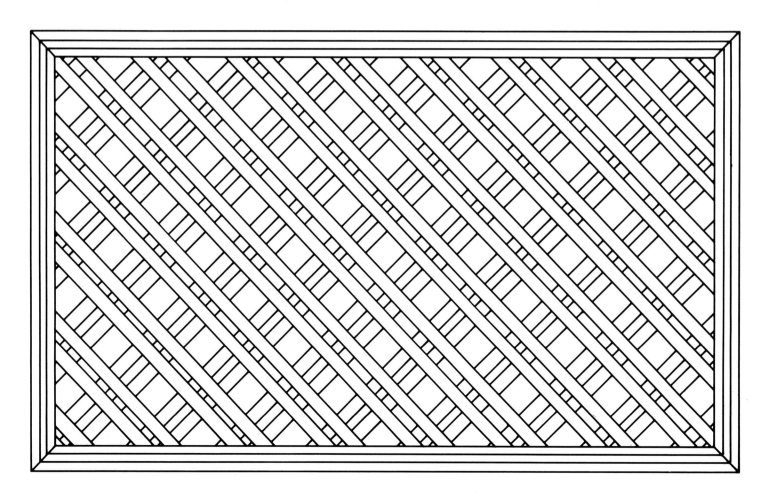

CONSTRUCTION

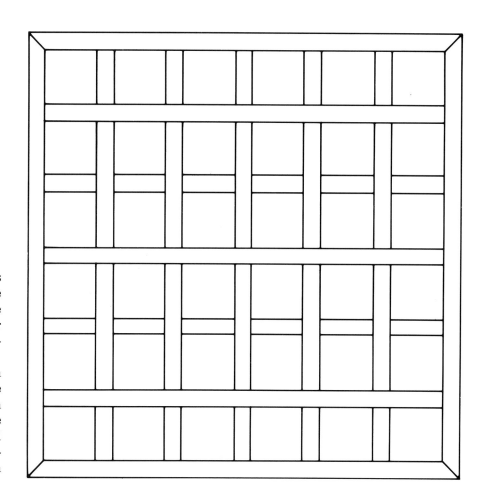

The appearance and longevity of one's trellis will undoubtedly benefit from care taken in construction. This is especially the case with wooden trellising, where poor techniques can produce unfortunate results.

Trellis is, by definition, composed of thin slats that are jointed where they cross. The joints of the trellised arbours in Roman gardens were bound by a variety of flexible materials. Twisted osiers, pliable hazel shoots, crude twine and fibres and the tendrils of climbers were seen on European

Great attention should be paid to the jointing of verticals and horizontals in the construction of trellis (above). Here horizontals and verticals are interwoven; turn this design 90 degrees to see the attractive effect of the same pattern set on the opposite axis.

Trellis-work, throughout much of its long history, has been woven or tied at its joints; pliable shoots and stems, fibrous material from herbaceous plants and simple twines were used as ties, a practice which could easily be restored today (right).

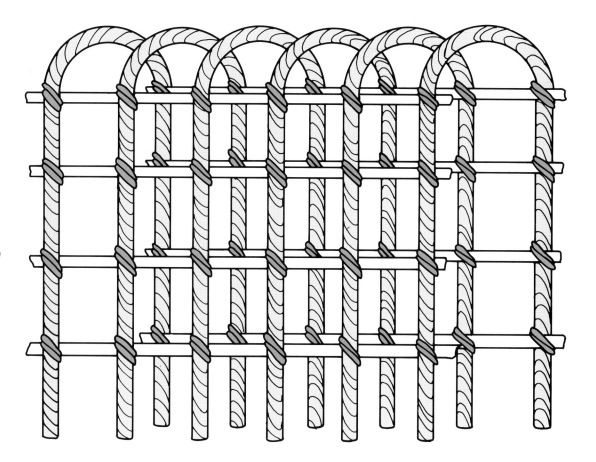

Some main joints must be carpented (opposite) both for structural reasons and appearance. The intricate detail required in ornate treillage (right) may inspire a level of craftsmanship similar to that of the cabinet-maker.

trellis until the seventeenth century and are still seen to this day in Japan (where they are either natural or artificially coloured). Nails and carpentry have been more common since, but there seems no reason why tied joints should not once again be used where the chosen material and style add to the artistry of the pattern.

Joints are intended to be a source of strength, but too often become a source of weakness, especially if there is no perimeter frame to the pattern. With some mass-produced trellis, the jointing is either infrequent and poor in execution, and the longer term consequence is further exacerbated where the wood is also thin or of poor quality. The common method for jointing trellis is with staples, either hammered in or fired in with a compressed air gun. There is nothing wrong with the method where it is comprehensive, subject to quality control and applied to good timber. But where this is not the case, the trellis ages faster than it should, especially when subject to pressure. (Inadequate joints can lead to immediate ageing where installation necessitates on-site carpentry in order to meet exact dimensions.) Some craftsmen, incidentally, insert

exterior wood glue to the joints prior to stapling. Properly carpented joints may be necessary on very heavy grades used in *treillage* effects, but are more common as an unseen feature of a structure's main timber frame. All staples, nails and screws should be galvanized.

External factors, too, play an important role in planning construction. Wind pressure and weight of planting can be judged and appropriate modifications made to a design at this stage. Any sort of a frame around one or more sides of a trellised pattern is, as we have seen, not only attractive but also considerably improves its basic resilience. This can be imperative with many modern diamond-meshes where the timber is thin and the jointing minimal. More pressure can be absorbed along the stronger ribs and joints of the frame rather than the fragile slats and lighter joints of the lattice. Timber rails across the middle of a pattern (but styled in the manner of a dado rail) and fixed securely at each end will also help.

Capping rails and plinths have the added benefit of serving (like post caps on uprights) to protect the main pattern from a large measure of falling and rising damp.

Preservatives and Surface Finish

The addition of appropriate preservatives and the correct application of a chosen finish are of the utmost importance to any material that is being put out in the garden or landscape. The time, money and effort involved in initiating such features, and the expectations demanded of them, justify a conscientious and careful approach.

The use of hardwoods attaches less urgency to pre-treatments and preservative finishes because of their inherent qualities for longevity as carpented timber. Softwoods, however, should where possible be pressure treated or 'tannalised', especially where the timber is in contact with the ground. The presence of constant moisture is exacerbated by the level of micro-biological activity present in soil, accelerating rotting and decomposition.

Some of the professional pre-treatments involve the use of chemicals that are highly toxic until the process is complete. Copper chrome arsonate, for instance, is one of the best treatments for timber prior to carpentry, or into which finished panels can be dipped; but it is lethal during the application when still wet, and needs a week in which to dry. Various timber treatments which involve less danger are available from DIY shops. Creosote is one of the more powerful but it suppresses plant life. Products such as 'Cuprinol' are better where shrubs and climbers are to flourish on and close to preserved timber. They provide significant (if not complete) protection to timber without affecting plant growth.

There have been considerable developments in exterior paints and stains, offering a wider choice of colours and more opportunities to coordinate finishes. The same colour can also be available with different constituents in order to cater for the nature of the material. This is appropriate for the separate needs of, for instance, wood, masonry and metal, as well as the variable absorption rates of different types of wood (prompting different concentrations of colour pigment).

Paints appropriate for most surfaces can be subject to marginal adjustments of hue, an exercise that is not uncommon given the variation between colour chart sample and finished effect. One can mix in a paint stain before application or between coats.

Many of the paints especially developed for exterior use boast 'micro-porosity'. This is apparently useful in the production of more intense colours, but more significant in that it allows the passage of air but not of water. The latter characteristic gives the

paint flexibility in order to cope with temperature-related expansion and contraction without cracking or flaking. With both stains and paints there is an element of weathering that takes place, softening the impact of their original colour. This process is faster where water based products are employed, and where insufficient coats are applied. This may be a regrettable mistake, or it may be deliberate policy in pursuit of a mellow effect in the shortest time. (Make sure the wood is properly pretreated, however.)

Another factor that can alter colour, though more immediately, is the surface porosity of the wood. A rough sawn softwood absorbs more liquid at a greater speed, and in so doing sometimes affects the balance of the pigments. The likelihood of an imbalance is greater the more complex the composition of the paint or stain. Some green stains, for instance, can become dark, muted and almost colourless on very absorbent woods. Planed hardwoods, by contrast, usually have a very low and slow absorption rate.

A word of warning on painting trelliswork at home. With a brush, it takes a very long time to do properly and, for those who have not tried it, the first coat can take twice as much time as was reckoned for two or three coats. Paint guns, and machines that spray it on with compressed air, are effective where the nozzle can cope with the thicker quality of many exterior paints. Do not be too optimistic, however, whatever you are told down at your local plant hire store. The quickest method is dipping, but for home production runs and small workshops, this can be impractical to set up in the space available. Dipping can also leave noticeable drip lines. The surest method, unfortunately, is the longest method, with a brush (and a roller where feasible).

Stains do not present these problems to anything like the same extent, being easier and quicker to apply. Care should still be taken, as they can still leave drip, run and splash marks. These can be hard to conceal as touching up often leaves permanently deeper shades, their effect being of an extra coat. Tempting as it is to speed up the process of getting the trellis up in the garden, apply the required number of applications and remember to allow all methods the recommended time to dry, both between coats and before being exposed to the elements. A few hours patience could make the difference of a few years in service. Incidentally, even where stains have been absorbed and drying for the correct amount of time, it is advisable to wear gloves when handling the trellis and uprights as a damp residue remains until they are weathered.

A painted finish (opposite) may involve more effort in its application and appear to weather more rapidly; but while in good condition it can project the line and detail of a design with a crisp, sharp impact. Stained finishes (left) are easier to apply and project softer tones that are often flattered by the mellowing effects of weather and time.

INSTALLATION

Wall-tops and Fence-tops

However prudent the choice of material and finish, poor installation and fixing can court disaster. The chosen procedure must reflect both the prevailing conditions of the site and the function intended of the trellis within those conditions. Its most common role in today's landscape is along boundary walls and fences, creating additional height and (where climbers are encouraged) screening. The dead weight of the trellis itself is obviously important, but there are a number of other factors that invariably justify sturdy anchoring and fixing.

As a barrier to the outside world, it is more than likely that climbers and tall shrubs, usually of some vigour, will be encouraged. The anticipated weight of intended planting as it matures is a factor for which allowance can easily be made at installation; it is much more difficult in retrospect.

There is also the likely pressure exerted by wind on both trellis and climber to be

taken into consideration, especially where the plants produce widespread cover.

The combination of height, plant cover, their combined weight and wind must not be under-estimated. Trellis-work by itself acts as an effective wind shield by stemming and filtering its force (and hence its use by some plantsmen as a 'string vest' around tender plants in the winter). Trellis with climbers, however, presents a much more solid profile, stopping the wind more suddenly by blocking its force. Such pressure can exert considerable leverage and strain on the fixings, especially if the trellis is heavy.

Take as comprehensive and as long a term view of fixings as possible. If wood uprights are being used, three inches by three inches timber gives much greater rigidity than two inches by two inches. The length the upright runs down the wall is important: at least one and a half times the depth of the trellis should be the absolute minimum where there is an appreciable amount of wind and/or intended planting. Do not rely on an absolute minimum, though. Err on the long side.

Where the walling below is in good condition, the uprights can be fixed into the masonry with bolts or screws at least six inches long. Avoid slim screws with a shallow thread in favour of heavier grades with a sharp thread. Wall plugs are essential. Such an operation is eased with an electric drill and two drill bits, one for wood and one for masonry.

Fixing the uprights can be both time-consuming and, when it comes to tightening up screws, tiring. It is worth persevering and aiming to get the job done as securely

There are a number of different methods for securing wall-top trellis. Lightweight uprights (opposite) rely for rigidity solely on the walling via screws or bolts. Where more weight or pressure is anticipated, or where the walling is in poor condition, additional strength can be achieved by the use of larger and longer uprights embedded in the ground below the wall (with or without a bedding of concrete). The latter technique (left) can be rendered even more effective by the use of pointed steel post sockets.

Whether flat to the wall, wall-top or both (opposite), the versatility of trellis is rarely limited by the means of fixing. On the left the wall is effectively heightened by a screen of trellis fixed to the whole height of the wall for solidity. The trellis on the back wall, the side of a building, need only be secured for part of the way of its total height.

Fencing can be given visual variety by the addition of trellis–work strips (below); the effect may be made even more interesting by the training of climbers through the lattice.

as possible right at the start. Trellis-work that capsizes into the garden four years later makes a sorry sight.

Of especial concern are the consequences of trellis being secured to deteriorating masonry or less than stable fencing. All the above precautions can be pursued, but however correct the dimensions of uprights and technique of fixing, cracked brickwork and crumbling pointing will allow the whole structure to move sideways (and down) with the wind. Ironically, the better the fixing in these circumstances, the more likely it is that the trellis will take some or all of the walling or fencing with it.

The approach that is best adopted is that of a longer upright sunk into the ground, with rather lighter fixings to the wall or fence. One method of gaining the depth in the ground is with a steel post socket. This should accommodate the bottom of the upright with a tight fit before tapering down to a sharp point, the overall length in the ground being either 24 inches or 36 inches. A special tool enables the socket to be set at the base of the wall first, before the upright. If the ground is soft, the socket can be set in concrete for extra rigidity. Steel sockets

should eliminate the need or temptation to sink 'untannalised' wooden uprights straight into the ground, with or without concrete sleeves. Not only do the sockets produce strength through depth, but they prevent the rotting that is inevitable where wood is permanently absorbing damp and the micro-biological activity present in soil particles.

One further option with a wall that is known to be weak involves the fixings between itself and the upright. Instead of bolts or screws, six inch nails can be driven into wall plugs. The stability for the trellis overhead is rooted downwards into the 36 inches of steel (and even concrete) below ground. If the combination of wind and weight is such that the trellis moves or comes down completely, it will not necessarily bring down the wall as well. The nails securing the upright to the masonry may just move within, or out of, their plugs without exerting too much pull on the wall.

In some instances, uprights can be fixed directly on to the top of a wall with flat-bottomed sockets or right-angle brackets. The masonry must be in good condition, and the finished effect must be able to cope

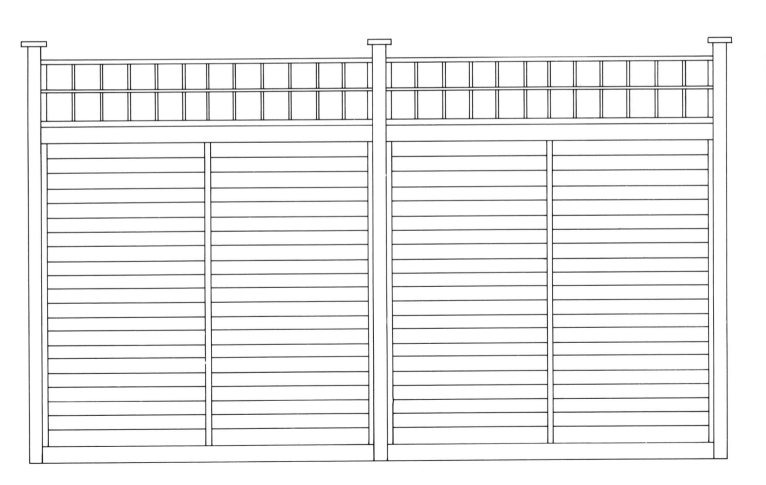

with sideways pressure. In these circumstances, cross-piece timbers can add to the strength of the structure. The most useful will be a capping rail that can be fixed securely at both ends and at all joints or uprights in between. The trellis-work can be secured to it along its length. A bottom rail, or plinth, would also help, as would any intermediate cross-pieces.

Flat to wall

Trellis that is destined to be installed flat to a wall or fencing can be fixed at as many points as necessary. Where it is decorative and light-weight, and free of heavy climbers, it can be held in place with relatively light attachments. Spacing blocks between the trellis and wall are, however, recommended, either in the shape of chocks of

wood or from less likely sources such as old cotton reels. Metal brackets or a network of timber battens can also be used to secure the trellis an inch or more out from a wall or fence behind.

The advantages of setting the trellis off from the wall in this way are notable. From a design angle, the depth between the trellis and wall can create a much more pleasing effect of light and shadow. The air that can circulate behind trellis-work also improves the performance of any climbers chosen, reducing the likelihood of some diseases and increasing the room for manoeuvring up and through the mesh. The health of the wall will also be improved, the more the trellis is kept clear the less it can act as a permanent source of damp which can travel through into the masonry; the trellis-work will also benefit from the drying effects of circulating air. Finally, any maintenance that is required, especially to

Twin layers of battens are an attractive and effective method for securing diamond-mesh flat to a wall (right). The cross-section shows the inner layer of battens fixed to the walling, the outer layer of battens fixed in exactly the same configuration as the inner layer, with the trellis held in between. The result could easily resemble the wall plan (far right), where pattern and proportion are introduced to a flat wall, as are depth and shadows.

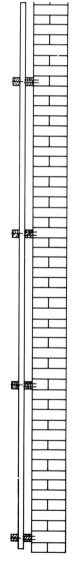

the wall, which may need to be treated or painted at intervals, can be easier. An electric drill, masonry screws and wall-plugs will all be needed.

Fixing trellis along the railings or coping that surround many roofs and balconies may involve some unorthodox initiative, depending upon the circumstances. Hard and fast rules do not apply, though one approach is the use of capping, plinth and dado rails throughout; they should be firmly jointed at any corners and their ends securely fastened to the house walls. Other uprights can perhaps be bracketed or socketed. Against railings, there is often the opportunity to use clips or, if necesary, wire. The latter should be as thick and as strong as possible, but in the interests of appearance remember that wire can be found in different colours, so that it can be matched to either the railings or the woodwork.

The design and fixing of flat-to-wall trellis-work are subject to lower structural requirements than wall-top or free-standing trellis. Thus it has traditionally attracted both greater and more delicate flights of fancy. The trompe-l'oeil (right) is well-balanced by the planting below and the architectural detail above; it would benefit by the masking of the brickwork where it runs behind the illusory perspective. This elaborate scheme (below) would be ideal against a rendered wall, which would save its elaborate detail and lavish illusion from any counter-pattern behind.

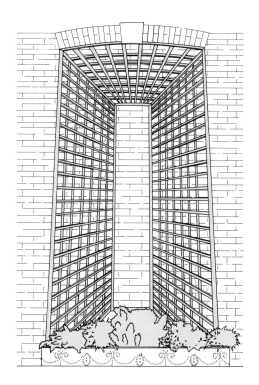

Free-standing

The provision of strength and stability from well below ground level is imperative with free-standing trellis, be it screening panels, arches or gazebos. The use of steel sockets, as just described, is one obvious method, and remains an invaluable weapon for the gardener and contractor.

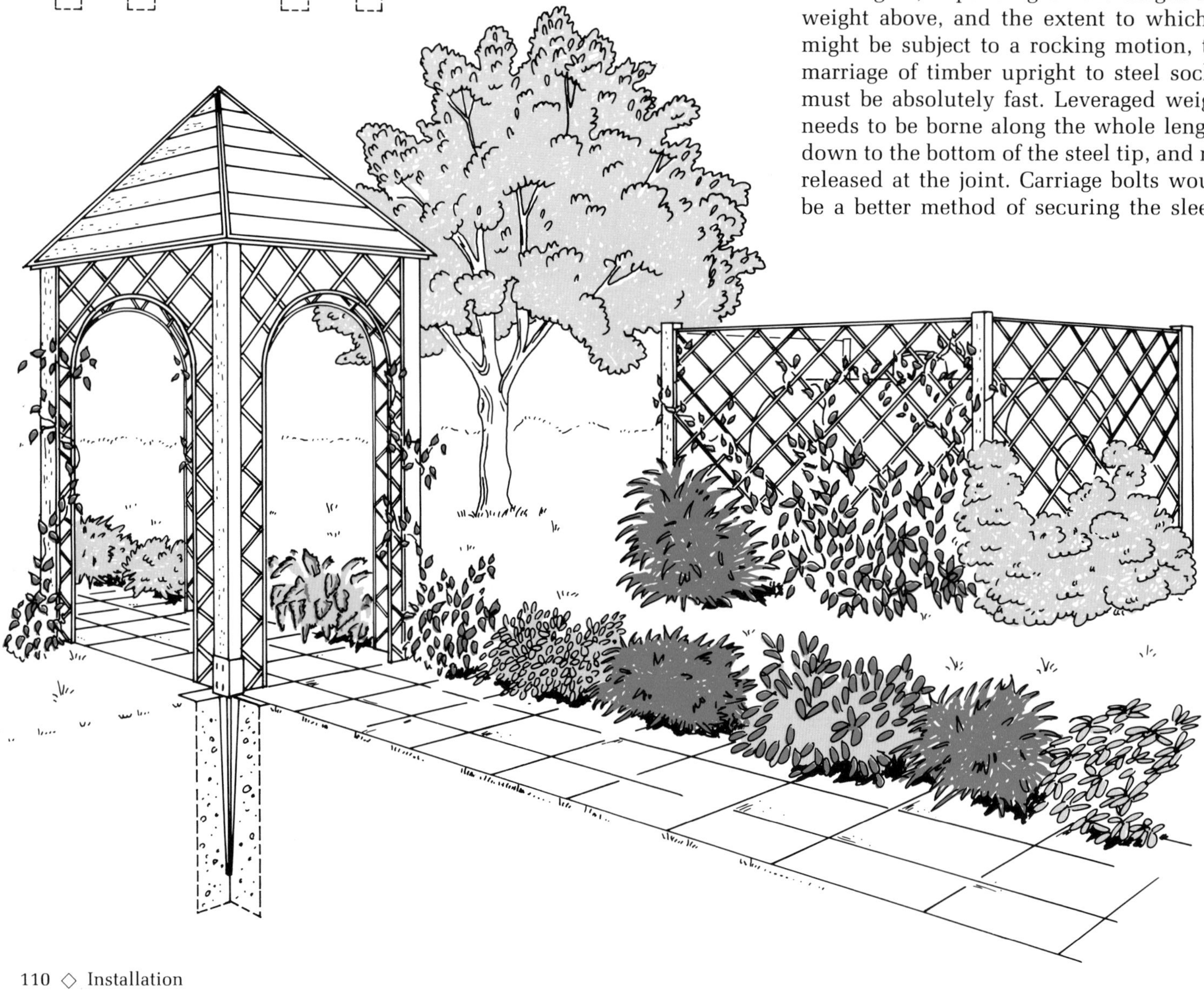

There can, however, be problems associated with sockets where there is no other means of additional support. Depending upon the dimensions of the structure above, and the extent to which it will exert leveraged weight at the bottom of the uprights, the sleeve into which the upright is inserted is not always long enough. Nor are the facilities that sockets offer for fitting around the base of the upright always effective. Many offer one or two small eyes in the steel sleeve through which a nail or small screw can be driven into the wood. Once again, depending on the height and weight above, and the extent to which it might be subject to a rocking motion, the marriage of timber upright to steel socket must be absolutely fast. Leveraged weight needs to be borne along the whole length, down to the bottom of the steel tip, and not released at the joint. Carriage bolts would be a better method of securing the sleeve around the timber upright for maximum stability.

The other variations that can be employed involve supplementary concreting and/or abandoning the socket in favour of properly 'tannalised' wooden uprights down to a similar or greater depth. In some situations, steel sockets are specifically avoided. Where, for instance, there is wide public access and a fear of vandalism, a steel socket without any secondary fixing (such as concrete or bolts) can cause worry in that a straight pull up can remove both it and the upright.

The last precaution to bear in mind is that when one is setting the socket, maintaining a perfect alignment to the vertical can be a challenge. 'Dollies' (short sections of wood that fit into the sleeve and have a steel cap that can take the blow of a sledge hammer) are available to assist driving the socket into the ground; but it is a good idea to pause at regular intervals to insert temporarily the required post and check the angle of the socket with a spirit level. Once the socket has lost its alignment, corrective pressure must be applied to it by a second pair of hands while the next blow is dealt, or the socket must be raised back to true and driven back down. Once it is established below ground, however, it may take considerable persuasion for it to adopt a new position.

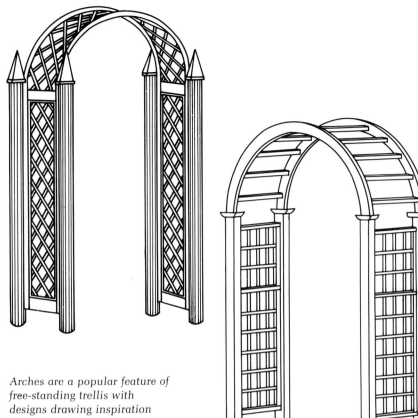

Arches are a popular feature of free-standing trellis with designs drawing inspiration from a wide range of different sources (above and below). Make sure that the screws and nails used in their construction are galvanized against rusting and that the timber is properly treated.

Echoing the shady bowers of earlier centuries, the simple structure (opposite above left) could be constructed from galvanized wire-netting on a frame of metal rods fixed into metal tubes set in concrete in the ground. The basic shape could be varied, the final effect being one of a densely planted arbour (opposite above right).

This decorative, open-sided structure (opposite below) consists of four uprights set into post sockets and concrete, arches within a trellised surround on each side, and a roof that can be either solid or latticed. Beyond is a suggestion for screening an oil-tank around three of its sides.

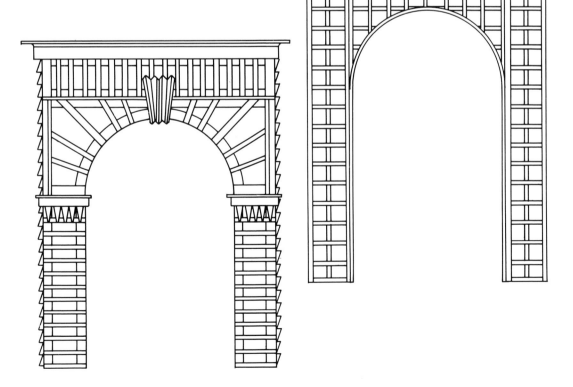

MAINTENANCE

Administering vital first-aid to ailing trellis-work or its fixing can be a time-consuming nightmare. Even more frustrating is that one's efforts can be surprisingly ineffective and short-lived. Disintegrating trellis mesh, broken or rotting uprights and loose fixings are difficult to rectify and awkward to tackle with a piecemeal approach once everything is established. If one upright or panel has to come down, the stress caused to both surrounding wood-work and planting can create further problems.

The easiest advice to give on the maintenance of trellis is that it is worth getting the job done as well as possible at the very

beginning. Where the right material has been properly constructed, where it has been successfully preserved and finished, and where, above all, it has then been solidly installed, its natural life span will be greater and the maintenance required of it will be less. Poor materials and installation can become a false economy, and a source of protracted irritation.

Superb as the initial construction and erection may be, however, both timber and metals will benefit from some attention. Many of the paints, stains and high-street preservatives, depending on the number of coats applied, begin to show their age after three or four years. Repeating the treatment may be desirable for the sake of appearance, but it will also renew endurance to the continual effects of weathering as well. Where the pre-treatment and/or quality of the material underneath are suspect, further applications will pay undoubted dividends. This is especially the case on those areas that are subject to the most stress, either from ground moisture, weight or leverage. Uprights are invariably worth a regular check as they are not only susceptible to both sources of stress but are also vital to the well-being of the remainder. They can be infuriating to replace singly without undue disturbance to adjacent trel-

The better the initial materials, construction, installation and finish, the less onerous and exhausting is the subsequent maintenance. These panels and uprights (right) are in western cedar, 'tannalised' where they are in contact with the ground and treated with preservative before being finished with two coats of stain.

In older gardens, the well-being of trellis and other effects can be threatened by the state of the masonry to which they are attached. Where a wall requires remedial work (above) make sure such maintenance is carried out before the installation of the final design. Ensure, too, that the paint chosen for all parts of the installation is suitable both for exterior use and for the material in question.

This angle of a contemporary piece of trellis-work (left) shows the careful attention to stong jointing necessary to long life and easy maintenance.

lising. Where such a task appears impossible, secondary supports are sometimes used, angled in as joints or props to the principal structure. Rarely are they attractive, but there are situations where they represent the only feasible approach and with the clever siting of climbers or shrubs they can be discreetly handled. It is sometimes possible to drive a six-inch nail through an existing upright into the masonry behind, adding effective, albeit short-term, aid.

Downward damp and moisture can be rendered less damaging by the use of capping rails and post caps. Both slow the direct access of damp into the core of the material below, saving trellis and uprights from premature ageing. Such items can be replaced with comparative ease when required. Similarly, where trellising is resting against or on a surface that is prone to damp, a rail or cross-piece will provide some defence and be easier to renew singly and deftly. Also simple in their replacement are the spacers or ribs that are recommended for trellis erected flat to a wall. They significantly reduce maintenance and increase life-expectancy by encouraging the passage of air around the wood (and brick) work; this helps dry any damp from both and reduces its passage from one to the other.

Very often, it is not the trellis, and its supports and fixings, that are suffering, but the structure to which it is attached. This is especially the case with older garden walls. Masonry can perhaps be repointed, and uprights can be renewed but set to a greater depth (either in concrete and/or metal sockets – make sure the timber is 'tannalised'). Really serious problems, however, may require the attention of a builder.

The maintenance of trellis-work is not always the easiest chore to execute in a comprehensive fashion and access can be difficult where part or all of it is planted with climbers. It should at least be attempted, though, given the time, effort and costs involved in its complete replacement, not to mention the visual effect on the garden of such an operation. If substantial renewal is necessary, and climbers are at risk, approach the job with patience and optimism. It is often practical to pivot a tangle of old trellis and planting flat to the ground, erect its replacement, patiently cut free and retrieve the climbers from the remains below, and restore them to the new mesh.

Where effective design, construction and maintenance produce longevity, garden structures become increasingly attractive as they mellow with the passage of time. Age lends a distinguished air to this spacious pergola (left) which has had the advantage of excellent specifications, including the freedom from ground moisture, which the raised walling prevents from reaching its uprights.

SPECIAL PROJECTS AND APPLICATIONS

The unusual development illustrated here caused a kitchen extension to intrude into the next-door garden and its windows to span the party wall, depriving the garden of any privacy. Knowing that the garden-owner was seeking a drastic solution, the neighbour took legal advice and threatened to invoke the 'Right of Light' to prevent screening across or unduly close to the kitchen window. The brief was, therefore, challenging: to devise attractive (and preferably instant) screening sufficient to create some privacy for the rest of the garden, but without causing offence to the neighbour. Trellis proved to be the perfect medium, and once the plan was complete, with rampant roses and a statue, neighbourly relations improved significantly.

FREE-STANDING ARCHES

The garden as was (opposite above) showing the window overlooking the neighbour's garden; this prompted a basic concept (opposite below left) which was both elegant and unobtrusive. The initial plan (opposite below right) was then submitted to all parties for approval, before adding the final details.

This plan (below) shows the scheme on completion, except the extent of the planting. The climbing roses at the base of each upright will provide thick cover on the trellis above and additional screening around the arch. The paving is lifted

and planted and the scene centred on an elegant statue of a goddess rising out of artemisias.

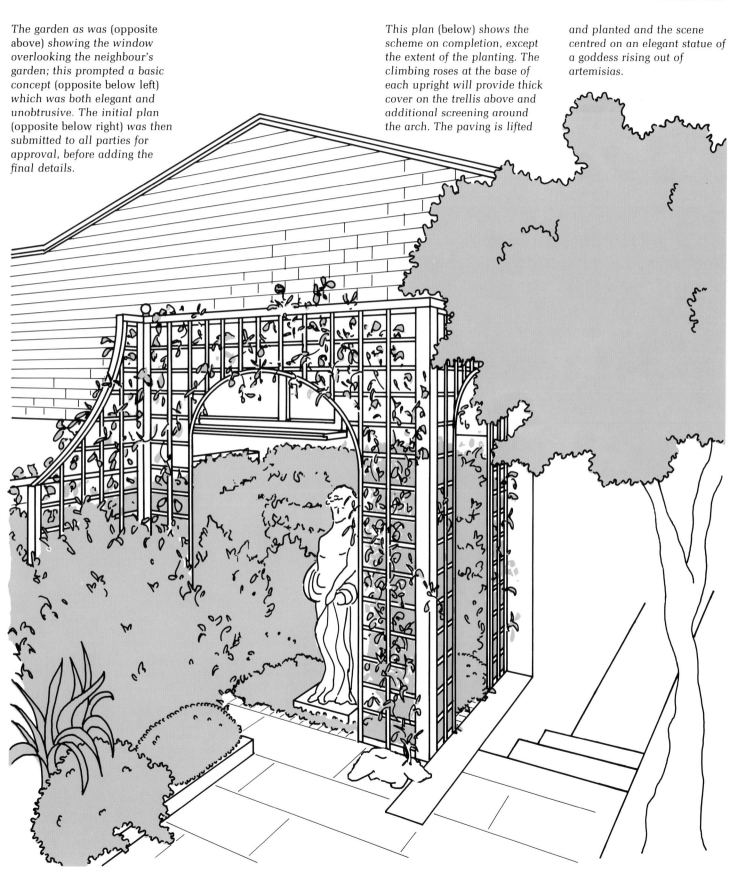

The brief that initiated these designs was for an arbour to complement a 200-year-old wisteria in a spacious central city garden. The majestic presence of the wisteria made the client's preference for *chinoiserie* styling all the more appropriate. Two contrasting ideas were submitted and during their conception it became obvious that whichever was chosen should ideally have the twisting trunk of the venerable wisteria woven immediately through its structure and lattice at installation. Thus, much of the assembly was done on site. The arbour was carpented in western redwood cedar (with its long-lasting weather tolerance) and left 'in the white' (i.e. untreated) so that the tones to which its natural grain mellows could complement the gnarled texture of the wisteria. The fixings are in copper, both for its resilience and its emerald tints once exposed to the elements.

FREE-STANDING PAVILIONS

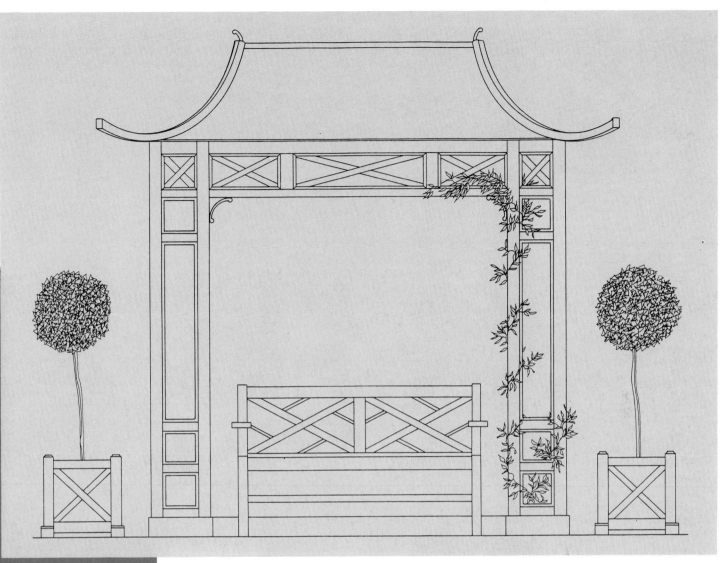

Unashamedly Oriental in style, both schemes sought an element of contemporary expression in the detailing and incorporated nearby planters. One design (above) was open-sided and gracefully proportioned, its solid roof (in lead or zinc) curving up to a flat top that echoes the back of the bench below. The other design (left) is more intimate, with the seat set back against a panel of rectangular trellis. Its peaked roof of open cross-pieces is, however, more dramatic as it arches up to a central finial. This latter concept prompted a design (right) which was pressed into indoor service before being promoted to the garden.

The need to modify the bleak effect of the back wall (opposite right) was sufficient motivation to undertake this trellis end-piece (right). Around a trompe-l'oeil of a Tuscan scene, a trellised canopy, seemingly supported by columns, appears to cross the garden in the style of a pergola which is echoed by the structure of the terrace in the foreground of the trompe. From the house, the columns and their simple trellised arches frame illusory windows that look out to the same view. Rosa 'Albertine', planted on each wing, has now covered much of the trellised canopy, softening its leading edge; and the artist has depicted Wisteria sinensis cascading down from the imaginary trellis beyond. The scene is made more dramatic by night with spotlights artfully recessed behind the large supporting cross-piece set on the columns; the lighting is restricted solely to soft effects thrown back on to the trompe, making the columns and trellised arches appear as black silhouettes.

A GARDEN END-

An enthusiastic builder, while renovating a house, completely bisected the owner's garden along its length with this blue slate terrace. Its daunting breadth and unwavering line, reminiscent of an airport runway, rushed the eye in a split second to an abrupt halt on the featureless render of the back wall. Without lifting and relaying large sections of slate paving, a scheme was required that would both make the garden feel longer and provide an end-piece of sufficient strength and interest to conclude such a broad sweep. In deliberate contrast to the cooler tones of the slate, a Mediterranean end-piece was contrived with trellised arches and the trellised canopy of a pergola, linking columns, planting and an impressive *trompe-l'oeil*.

PIECE

This series of development drawings was prompted by the need to find an elegant solution to problems besetting a small city garden. Square in shape and paved, it was dominated on two sides by a backdrop of nearby multi-storeyed buildings and bounded on the third by the tall windowless back of a neighbour's house. The overriding need was to distract the eye from the oppressive surroundings and imbue the garden with its own independence and character.

FORMAL END-PIECES

The extent of these variations on an end-piece reflect both the garden owner's enthusiasm for treillage and the ease with which Classical proportions accommodate combinations of trellised pattern. This design (above) was eventually chosen, but the raised bed was removed and the tree dropped to ground level. The two flanking walls had panels

based on a variant design
(opposite left below). The
garden was completed with an
acacia tree planted central to
the square to provide a focal
point. Its height complemented
the scale of the panels, while
its airy lines and feathered
foliage cast light shadows,
contrasting with the precise
detailing of the treillage.

On both the terraces illustrated here, overlooking windows threatened the extent to
which they could be enjoyed as gardens. It
remained important, however, that the pursuit of seclusion did not lead to trellis-work
so extensive and monotonous as to produce
a feeling of imprisonment. These designs
had, therefore, to combine style and personal preference with a deft but strategic
response to specific problems. The Moorish
fantasy, off a denlike sitting room, and the
Art Nouveau profile, set between a drawing
room and a bedroom may seem slightly
improbable at first sight, but both schemes
provide an attractive counterpoint to a
bland architectural setting and unremark-
able urban skyline.

*The flowing profile (left) and
the positioning of the tree
correspond to the location of
neighbouring windows. With
uprights outside the railings,
white diamond-mesh was
chosen both to emphasize the
form of the top rail and to
provide deliberate contrast to
the upright railings. This
end-piece (above) has arches
set 15 inches forward of a
panel of diamond-mesh.*

ROOF TERRACE AND PATIO

The on-site sketch (below) picks out the two features to form the basis of a face-lift: the walled-up arches and upper edge of the lower section. The final design, (opposite) is seen in cross-section (right) with the diamond-mesh arches set away from the walling but secured with cross-pieces.

Dominating the back door of a Palladian house was a long curving expanse of drably rendered walling that reached windowless from the tarmac below to the cornice running along the roof line. The fact that this was the most frequently used entrance to the housing prompted this scheme to improve the prospect by exploiting two previously insignificant features. The upper section, below the cornice, was marginally recessed, suggesting two tiers of pattern, while the still visible outline of walled up arches at ground level provided a theme for the lower tier. The final design incorporated diamond-mesh arches stepped out from the wall by the width of the square planters, masking their otherwise awkward presence, creating recessed arches, with all the interesting aspects of off-set trellis, notably the play of shadow on the wall behind. The pattern above, in deliberate contrast, was in a sedate rectangular mesh.

A HOUSE WALL

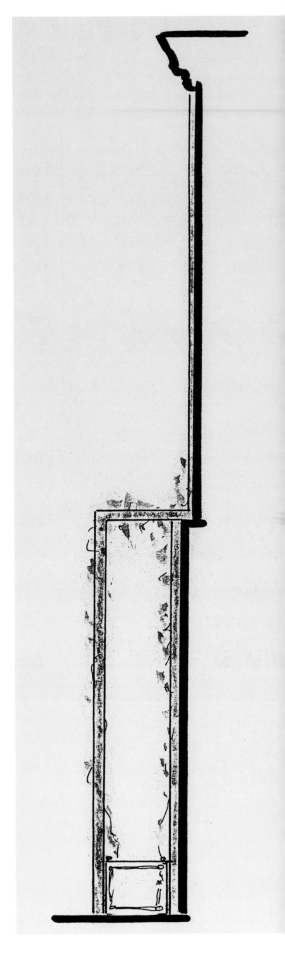

With imagination, basement wells can be transformed into small courtyards. The project on this page was for the middle of an early nineteenth-century house with stucco walls rising two to four storeys on each side. The atmosphere was gloomy and there was no temptation to step out through the french windows. The trellised scheme shown, with planting, paving, seat and night lighting, exploited the compact dimensions and bleak walling, the vacant gloom replaced with pattern and intimacy. The well in the illustrations opposite, while more spacious, is still flanked by taller buildings. The owners were keen to explore ideas on paper, one with associations of the Moorish courtyard with a mosaic floor pattern and tight diamond-mesh, the other more Classical and sedate. Subtle lighting within the trellised recesses ensured it could be enjoyed after dark.

The depth of the well (below) reduced the amount of light reaching the white stucco walls. The trellis was therefore specified in untreated western red cedar for its pale tones. The better light enjoyed in the other well (opposite above and below), permitted these two schemes to be designed in dark green.

BASEMENT WELLS

CHAPTER
FOUR

PLANTING
AND
TRELLIS

*There should be a harmony of
pattern and mood between
trellis and planting that
enhances the appearance of
both. Here, the elegance and
rhythm of the trellis-work
combines with the form, foliage
and flower of a climbing rose
to provide a superb prelude to
the statue beyond.*

GENERAL PRINCIPLES

Different styles of trellis are suited to different styles of planting, and vice versa. Ideally, the association should flatter both elements. The shape and character of a *Rosa* 'Albertine' may be perfectly set off by the pattern (and perhaps colour) of the trellis; the architecture and flow of the trellis can be set off by close integration with the rose trees, losing the awkwardness that can afflict conspicuously man-made contrivances in largely natural settings.

In most gardens (especially in urban situations) and in most roles, trellis benefits from complementary planting, even if the two are kept totally separate. Trellis is, after all, an architectural element set against a backdrop that is dominated either by nature or by a profusion of further architecture. Its presence and purpose may need emphasis.

Two characteristics of potential companions should be remembered. The first is their overall vigour and profile. Some trellis-work, depending upon its design and role, calls for heavy cover. Crude, plodding mesh can appear uneasy, spoiling the garden over which it hovers and little better than the background it may be screening. Similarly, the imbalance may be reversed where attractively styled trellis looks incongruous against the proportions and detail of other features. In both cases, the anonymity afforded by a thick climber can be directed at the offending element, softening its impact. Beware, however, the situation where the inherent character of trellis and surrounds needs only the lightest planting.

Plants also impart their own tapestry of tone and texture, pattern and shadow.

There is, theoretically, a wide spectrum on offer, from the dark, glossy and large-leafed to the pale, delicate and feathery. Where style and colour are ingredients of the trellis and its surrounds, remember that foliage, flowers and possibly fruits will improve the overall picture. Achieving the perfect association can, in practice, be challenging, since choice of climber or shrub may be restricted by planting conditions.

Also frustrating, and not unusual in built-up areas, is for one's own efforts to be undermined by a neighbour. Intrusive plants from an adjoining garden can run riot across trellis for which a more composed scheme had been conceived. Similarly, neighbours can harbour bindweed, the nightshade clan and other weeds that seldom miss an opportunity for social climbing.

The pattern and shadows of a cascading wisteria against close-set diamond-mesh (opposite) bring movement and drama to an architectural composition of lead ornament and brickwork. The bold dimensions and styling of these trellised panels (above) will be further improved when the associated planting becomes fully integrated with the lattice.

One of the most effective uses of trellis is in combination with garden statuary and planting; this arrangement of a bust in a trellised niche will improve considerably as a nearby ivy of notable vigour spreads outwards to soften the intensity of the diamond-mesh.

General Principles ◇ 133

HEAVY COVER

Ivy (below) and jasmine (right) can both provide rapid and thick cover to trellis-work. The jasmine, in this instance, is best subject to some control. While screening is needed, the architectural character and detail of the trellis should remain an obvious and dynamic undercurrent within foliage, rather than being obscured completely.

Trellis-work can be the vehicle for substantial planting for a number of different reasons. One of the most common is the need for the trellis to serve as a screen. This could be external, along a boundary, or internal, where it might be either fundamental to a garden's lay-out or a countermeasure against such unsightly necessities as oil-tanks. The gardener may have other reasons, trellis being the practical means and perfect excuse for the display of climbers and tall shrubs.

Frequently, the trellis itself needs a degree of cover to achieve its full effect. Inappropriate styling, or a complete absence of it, is best masked with exuberant planting. The weight and shape of a trellised structure may be inappropriate or downright ugly; its impact may be absurd, disappointing or depressing, and wholly inconsistent with the potential of the setting and intention of the owner. Some trellis is so blatantly functional in line and uncompromising in character that, rather than being an embellishment to a garden, it actually disturbs its atmosphere. This can easily happen in many modern gardens where space is at a premium, yet the need to create a pleasant, secluded place is as great as the need for screening. A jungle of thick climbers and shrubs can bring welcome concealment to the cruder meshes.

When planning deliberately heavy planting, keep in mind the eventual weight and outline of the chosen candidates. An endearing little plant labelled 'vigorous' in the garden centre may, despite its air of innocence, develop into an uncontrollable aggressor. The Russian vine, *Polyganum baldschuanicum*, is one of the most notorious, growing up to twenty feet a year and smothering everything in its path with a tangle of thick undergrowth; the only view that will remain of any trellis-work will be the feet of the uprights. Also disappearing into the advancing jungle will be other plants, nearby structures and neighbouring buildings. Ivies and virginia creepers, where they are unchecked, can also invade surrounding spaces and effects.

The prudent use of vigorous climbers and shrubs can otherwise be very successful, especially if the trellis is used in a screening role. Subject to control, ivies and creepers, *Akebia quinata*, *Clematis montana* and *armandii*, and most honeysuckles are suitable. The more rampant roses, jasmines, *Caenothus* and *Philadelphus* will also be appropriate. All these can create a fairly thick barrier, making the most of the mesh provided. If the secateurs are wielded now and then, not only will overall proportions be kept in balance, but a hint of trellis-work can also be retained,

With little more than the uprights of a heavily planted pergola hinting at the unseen trellis-work overhead and along one side (right), profuse foliage is shaped and sculpted to lead the eye on further.

not as a bleak pattern, but sufficient to spice the thick tangle with an undercurrent of architectural symmetry.

When planting climbers in combination with roof and balcony trellis, it is important to take into account the draughty conditions in which climbers are expected to flourish. To establish good growth on any trellis that is frequently exposed to wind, and especially where the plants are grown from the restricted root runs of pots, containers and raised beds, constant attention or a small irrigation system may be needed. Both plants and soils need more moisture on roof tops and balconies as they lose it faster. Such irrigation systems, including a compact computerised device that will water on a pre-set cycle, can be easy to install and are surprisingly affordable. They have a noticeable and rewarding impact on resulting growth. Without sufficient moisture, climbers intending to scale trellis in the face of constant draughts can look emaciated and fail to perform their allotted duties.

CLIMBERS SUITABLE FOR PROVIDING HEAVY TRELLIS COVER

Local conditions, above and below ground, are one of a number of factors that affect the typical growth of a plant. Thus the lists below should be treated as being a broad guide rather than definitive. Two climbing families, *Clematis* and *Lonicera* (honeysuckle) are generally at their best where their roots are in shade while their top growth is in good light.

Climbers which thrive in full sun

Evergreen and Semi-evergreen	Deciduous
(Semi-evergreen refers to those plants that keep many of their leaves in milder and more protected sites.)	Actinidia chinensis Ampelopsis species Chaenomeles speciosa (Flowering Quince or Japonica)
Clematis armandii	Clematis flammula
Clematis meyeriana	Clematis montana
Elaeagnus × ebbingei	Clematis viticella (some)
Euonymus fortunei radicans and cultivars	Humulus lupulus (Hop)
Hedera species (Ivies)	Hydrangea petiolaris (Climbing Hydrangea)
Jasminum officinale	Ipomoea sp. and var.*
Lonicera henryi (Honeysuckle)	Lonicera tragophylla (Honeysuckle)
Lonicera japonica and cultivars	Polygonum baldschuanicum (Russian Vine)
Passiflora cearulea (Blue Passion Flower)*	Rosa (stronger climbers/ramblers)
Rosa Mermaid	Vitis species (Vines)
Solanum crispum	Wisteria floribunda
Solanum jasminoides (Potato Vine)	Wisteria sinensis
Trachelospermum jasminoides	

* Where winters are cold these plants should usually be given the warmest possible sites or, if herbaceous, be treated as annuals.

Climbers which thrive in semi-shade or full shade

Evergreen and Semi-evergreen	Deciduous
(Semi-evergreen refers to those plants that keep many of their leaves in milder and more protected sites.)	Actinidia chinensis* Ampelopsis (most species)* Chaenomeles speciosa* Clematis flammula*
Akebia quinata**	Clematis macropetela*
Clematis armandii*	Clematis montana**
Clematis meyeriana*	Clematis vitalba*
Elaeagnus × ebbingei **	Clematis viticella (some)*
Euonymus fortunei radicans and varieties**	Humulus lupulus aureus (Golden Hop)*
Hedera species (Ivies)**	Hydrangea petiolaris**
Jasminum officinale*	Lonicera caprifolium**
Lonicera henryi (Honeysuckle)*	Lonicera periclymenum and var.**
Lonicera japonica*	Lonicera × tellmaniana**
Lonicera sempervirens*	Lonicera tragophylla**
Trachelospermum jasminoides*	Parthenocissus quinquefolia (Virginia Creeper)**
	Parthenocissus species**
	Polygonum baldschuanicum (Russian Vine)*
	Rosa (some)*
	Vitis species (Vines)*
	Wisteria floribunda*

* Semi-shade only.
** Semi-shade or full shade.

LIGHT COVER

Open wands of the climbing rose 'Aimée Vibert' (opposite) leave a clear view of the carpented detail behind. The Magnolia grandiflora to its right will also help to improve the effect of this especially stylish trellis-work. A regularly pruned jasmine (below) and the shrubby Cytissus battandieri visible in the corner aim similarly to provide strong but deliberately incomplete cover.

The combining of climbers and other plants with architectural effects can pose certain problems. Effective screening may be needed from the planting, but the best possible effects are to be obtained from finding the correct balance between architectural pattern and natural form. This balance will be found through careful regard for outline, weight, detail, texture and tone.

The more vigorous types of ivy, clematis and rose remain eminently suitable for such planting but they must be subject to the necessary pruning and training. If left too much to their own devices, they will quickly take over the trellis-work, obliterat-

The elegant lines and upward sweep of this striking end-piece (above) remain uncluttered by the deliberately selective planting around its edges and in front of the arch.

ing its finer points from view. It is not uncommon to see attractive woodwork, full of artistry and pattern, smothered rather than complemented by vigorous climbers. With sufficient control, however, the inherent strength and presence of many of the climbers listed here can be harnessed to good effect, off-setting the form and design of stylised trellis-work. Architecture in the landscape only achieves its full effect when it relates to or contrasts with natural forms; the bolder the architecture, the bolder its context will need to be.

For this reason many shrubs, especially those known as 'wall' shrubs, are highly appropriate for controlled planting with trellis. Their simpler profiles can suggest solid buttresses, anchoring but flattering the flowing patterns and airy refinements of any trellising. Their depth also introduces a third dimension to an art form that often feels fixed in just two dimensions. In this role, yew, *Ceanothus*, camellias, magnolias and *Philadelphus* are just a few of the many candidates. Their effect contrasts noticeably with those climbers that have sprawling profiles and whose passage and shape are more closely governed by the two-dimensional form of the trellis itself. Not all 'wall' shrubs, however, are dark and tightly knit; acacias, *cytissus*, buddleias and others offer more relaxed shapes.

Where climbers are wanted which do not need constant attention, select those species and varieties that are either smaller or slower in habit. While *Clematis armandii* and *montana*, for instance, are notoriously vigorous, *Clematis macropetala, alpina,*

The simple charm and detail of these two rectangular-meshed designs (left and below) would be spoilt by robust or invasive planting. They would be ideally balanced by the flowers and foliage of more reticent partners, such as those roses and clematis that are attractive in habit and only moderate in vigour.

orientalis and the 'Jackmanii' hybrids can be delightfully displayed. Roses also offer considerable choice.

All plants show differing degrees of pattern and detail in their foliage. Therefore trellis-work which has an intricate pattern may be best complemented by climbers or shrubs which do not. The foliage of wisterias and some of the jasmines and clematis, for instance, combine very well with most trellis; but such harmony is less certain when they are used in conjunction with complex *treillage*. Foliage also imparts texture and tone, factors that could require careful handling where the finish of the trellis itself projects a specific mood or colour. As we saw earlier, a soft 'Monet green' finish does not go well with foliage of a similarly soft tint.

SHRUBS AND CLIMBERS SUITABLE FOR PROVIDING PARTIAL TRELLIS COVER

Shrubs and climbers which thrive in full sun

Evergreen and Semi-evergreen

(Semi-evergreen refers to those plants that keep many of their leaves in milder and more protected sites.)
Abelia × grandiflora†
Abutilon megapotamicum†
Acacia sp.†
Berberis darwinii
Berberis × stenophylla
Camellia sp. and var.
Ceanothus sp. and var.
Choisya ternata
Coronilla glauca
Cotoneaster (various)
Cytissus battandieri
Eccremocarpus scaber (Glory Vine)†*
Escallonia (various)
Euonymus fortunei radicans and var.
Hedera some sp. and var. (Ivies)
Hydrangea serratifolia
Magnolia grandiflora
Passiflora edulis (Passion Flower)†
Pelargonium peltatum (Ivy-leaved Geranium)†
Piptanthus laburnifolius (Evergreen Laburnum)
Pittosporum sp. and var.†
Pyracantha sp. and var.
Senecio scandens

Deciduous

Abutilon sp. and var.
Actinidia kolomikta
Buddleia sp. and var.
Campsis radicans (Trumpet Vine)†
Chaenomeles sp. and var.
Clematis × 'Jackmanii'
Clematis orientalis
Clematis viticella (some)
Cobaea scandens†
Cotoneaster horizontalis
Ipomoea (some)†
Jasminum nudiflorum (Winter Jasmine)
Lathyrus latifolius (Everlasting Sweet Pea)
Lathyrus odoratus (Annual Sweet Pea)
Magnolia (various)
Philadelphus sp. and var.
Plumbago capensis†
Rosa (various)
Schizophragma species (eventually large, but slow)
Tropaeolum speciosum (happiest where its roots are shaded)
Wisteria floribunda

* Control will certainly be necessary to prevent heavy growth.
† Where winters are cold these plants should be given the warmest possible site or, if herbaceous, be treated as annuals.

Climbers which thrive in semi-shade or full shade

Evergreen and Semi-evergreen

(Semi-evergreen refers to those plants that keep many of their leaves in milder and more protected sites.)
Abelia × grandiflora*†
Berberidopsis corallina**
Berberis darwinii*
Berberis × stenophylla*
Camellia sp. and var.**
Choisya ternata**
Cotoneaster (various)* or **
Eccremocarpus scaber (Glory Vine)*†
Euonymus fortunei radicans and var.**
Hedera (some) (Ivies)**
Hydrangea serratifolia**
Lonicera fragrantissima**
Lonicera japonica 'Aureo-reticulata'*
Pyracantha (various)**

Deciduous

Actinidia kolomikta*
Chaenomeles sp. and var.* or **
Clematis × 'Jackmanii'**
Clematis 'Lasurstern'**
Clematis macropetala*
Clematis 'Nelly Moser'**
Clematis viticella (some)*
Jasminum nudiflorum (Winter Jasmine)**
Rosa 'New Dawn' (and some others)*
Schizophragma species (eventually large, but slow)**
Tropaeolum speciosum*
Wisteria floribunda (some control necessary to prevent heavy growth)*

* Semi-shade only. ** Semi-shade or full shade.
† Where winters are cold these plants should be given the warmest possible site or, if herbaceous, be treated as annuals.

This trellis (opposite) has been left unplanted in its role as a subdued but rhythmic backdrop. It gives a distinct texture to the shadows behind a strong centre-piece of water, planting and statuary.

FOREGROUND PLANTING

The trellised arch (below) hardly needs climbers winding their way through its strong architectural form. It does, however, require strength both behind and in front; the dark depths beyond provide a suitable backdrop, while the foreground is filled in by pot planting.

To suggest that all trellis-work needs the immediate companionship of climbers would be misleading. *Treillage*, dramatic or elegant, can generate its own fascination with contrasting pattern, clever proportions and exuberant or delicate detail. The impact may not be enhanced at all where climbing plants are allowed to obscure such artistry. This has always been well understood in the Orient, where the beauty and symbolism of lattice is rarely confused or obscured by the counter-pattern of a climber. There has always been, however, a close and deliberate relationship between plant and panel. The Japanese garden designers, especially, have explored the potency of such associations, coordinating their fences and screens with conspicuously natural forms, without either necessarily touching the other – hence the frequent presence of contorted pine trunks and wisteria stems twisting cleanly through, behind or around lattice patterns.

Where trellis is a picture in its own right, in any tradition, plantsmen can, as in Japan, turn their attention to the wider setting. Creative trellis and *treillage* is often sited where it complements, or is being complemented by, the architectural mood of a foreground or backdrop. In this instance, the required planting may need to be similarly architectural in form, but refreshingly simple in its provision of contrasting line and texture. Thus the perfect foreground may consist of a bland surface (such as mown grass or terracing) with a pair of clipped or trained evergreens. Com-

mon box (*Buxus sempervirens*), English yew (*Taxus baccata*) or Holly (*Ilex species*) would be appropriate for the latter.

A number of plants present an orderly and neat appearance without the need of constant manicure. Many conifers fall into this category, as do some hebes, most camellias, and an assortment of other broad-leaved evergreens, such as the *Osmanthus* clan, which also includes *Osmareas* and *Phillyreas*. Their seemingly good behaviour is often a product of slow growth, so in favourable conditions their proportions will ultimately demand some attention.

As a prelude to picturesque trellis-work, there may be a need for some emphatic foreground planting. Evergreen species can often be clipped or standard specimens may be chosen, to make an architectural effect with their upright trunks and top growth. Often seen in this role are bay trees (*Laurus nobilis*), hollies (*Ilex species*) and the evergreen or holm oak (*Quercus ilex*).

Dramatic effects can be made with the pencil-thin proportions of some conifers,

ranging from the smaller junipers up to the Italian cypress (*Cupressus sempervirens*). Equally sharp-edged and dramatic, but altogether busier with their sword-like leaves exploding out from the centre, are such plants as the yuccas and phormiums.

The architectural treatment of foreground planting may also extend to the use of planters. This may be by choice, where the shape of a Versailles tub or the colour of a terracotta urn complements the trellis beyond; or it may be out of necessity, should there be no access to beds or plantable ground just where it is needed. In either event, it is worth being as careful with the association between planter and trellis work as it is between plant and trellis-work.

Treillage which justifies this very cautious and detached plantsmanship usually incorporates some sort of rhythm or focus in its design. It is in this that the purpose of foreground planting can lie. Any of the above schemes can be used to present and reinforce the pattern beyond; they may frame a central panel, or guide the eye along a sequence of panels; or they might

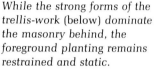

While the strong forms of the trellis-work (below) dominate the masonry behind, the foreground planting remains restrained and static.

imply that there is yet more to be seen from a different angle, an effect of mystery well worth creating even if it has no basis in reality.

The successful *trompe-l'oeil* in trellis is usually best treated as *treillage* where associated planting is concerned. Its own elaborate perspective should not be confused with incongruous and competitive pattern. The *trompe-l'oeil* will probably benefit, however, from being viewed through foreground planting and flanked by background planting. With the latter, remember that, as far as the *trompe* is concerned, the flanks and background are very often the middle ground to the illusory focus beyond.

There does, however, remain another option for the ambitious plantsman which involves training shrubs and climbers that are carefully selected and sited for the varying proportions of their foliage and their disciplined growth when cut. Suitable candidates include *Pyracantha* and the many different forms of ivy, but it can be hard work for what, at best, is likely to be an amusing contrivance.

With billowing foliage acting as a frame both above and below (right) it is not always necessary to obscure the pattern and detailing of the trellis-work in the middle.

PLANNING AND BUYING

With careful thought, the versatility and variety of trellis-work can enable stylish gardens to be created from the most unlikely sites.

SOURCES

Mass-produced Trellis

Most garden centres and DIY stores sell standard panels from wholesale producers. Simple square-meshes and expanding diamond-meshes are regarded as basic stock items; such trellis is usually finished in a brown stain and made from timber which has been subject to some sort of preservative treatment. Square- and diamond-mesh may also be available in a white (painted) finish. The quality of the material used in wholesale trellis and the levels of preservation, carpentry and jointing can vary from good to disappointing and must be carefully considered before purchase. A compromise may also have to be made between what is ideally wanted by an owner for the site and what is available as a mass-produced off-the-shelf item.

Garden centres and DIY stores invariably offer wooden 2 in. × 2 in. and 3 in. × 3 in. uprights as well, and while some of these will have been pressure-treated with a preservative (a pre-treatment that is highly recommended), this is not always the case. Although they may have been pressure treated, posts and uprights are often sold without a final stain. This can enable one to choose a tone that will match the finish of the trellis-work it is to hold. A finish should certainly be applied, even if colourless. Where post caps are also on offer, they are a very worthwhile but inexpensive addition in that they provide protection against weathering and a pleasing embellishment.

It is rare for a garden centre to offer as comprehensive a range of fixings as the DIY or hardware shops. To get trellis installed properly at the start, one may want to consider different types of steel socket, bracket, bolt, expanding bolt, screw, plug and nail. Advice may also be needed. Most DIY and hardware stores will, furthermore, have such useful aids as bags of dry but ready-mixed concrete which are easy to handle and ideal where only a small quantity is required.

Sources for both preservatives and finishes are varied. Garden centres usually carry those preservatives and stains that combine protection and some choice of colour without so much chemical that plant growth is jeopardised. DIY stores, builders' and timber merchants and the better paint shops tend to have a wider range with both exterior finishes for different materials in a choice of colours and some of the more toxic but highly potent treatments for preservation.

Post caps have already been mentioned, but there are other additions that will bene-

Mass-produced light-weight trellis can brighten up awkward areas, but sensible precautions must be taken. The square- and diamond-meshes (right above and below) were re-treated with preservative before being painted white. The basic quality of the timber and factory-made joints, however, were barely strong enough to withstand the on-site carpentry necessitated by the down-pipes and overall design. Remedial action and re-jointing were thus required from the beginning of the installation.

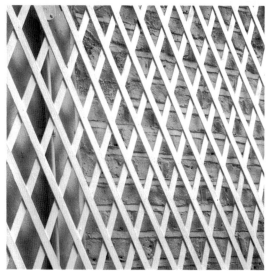

fit standard trellis designs. Some panels are made with a capping rail already in place though this is not normally the case. As with all rails above, in the middle and below panels of trellis mesh, they help to protect against the elements and provide a pleasing frame around the pattern. DIY stores and timber merchants should have the necessary lengths of timber, and some will be able to supply top rails with a suitable moulding that gives a slight peak or ridge along the centre of their upper side. Remember to treat all such additions with a preservative or finish.

Finials, plinths and other embellishments can be commissioned from joiners or made at home; they may also be sold as such by timber merchants, hardware shops and DIY stores, albeit as decoration for items such as staircase newels and curtain-pole ends. There are some standard ranges of round balls, acorns, pineapples and Gothic spikes. Otherwise, explore what is on offer in the way of large furniture knobs. For rounded finials of yet more spacious proportions, a limited order from a joiner might be expensive. Try any source of plumbers' ball-cocks for the balls. They will have to be painted as they are usually in plastic or fibre-glass, and this may be impractical where the rest of a trellised structure is to be stained. Where suitable, however, they remain one of the cheapest sources for the dimensions they offer.

Specialist Trellis

For the garden owner, whatever the situation, trellis can represent a considerable investment of time, money, effort and expectation. No form of trellis-work can be

Specialist trellis, whether commissioned or stock design, can respond with greater sensitivity to the needs of both site (below) and owner. Such designs as these should be realized in high-quality materials and workmanship to make a durable contribution to the overall architectural effect.

described as cheap, but some does undoubtedly represent much better value than others. Where it is mass-produced and widely distributed, too little of the price represents design or finish, while a significant amount accrues from handling and marking-up between the production and retail ends of the trade. The closer the buyer is to the craftsman, the more the price will represent material, artistry, detail and method.

Apart from design, one of the most compelling factors in the comparative value between different types of trellis is longevity, an asset that very often reflects its original level of craftsmanship. Replacing trellis-work once it is on site and in service is not only expensive but disruptive and difficult. As with any feature introduced to the garden, trellis-work should be able to tailor aspiration, taste and means to the needs of the site. It should not be a disappointing compromise but a source of pleasure and design, and value in every sense. The calibre and honesty of the craftsmanship, and the quality of the materials and method, are important.

The better the materials and initial carpentry, the easier subsequent improvisation. Shown bracketed straight on to brick coping, this design (below) demonstrates how on-site tailoring can be used to make the trellis-work combine with an uneven wall effect.

In built-up areas (right) successful garden design thrives on concise and convincing expressions of individuality. Specialist trellis-work, tailored to fit particularly awkward locations, can transform a garden or terrace, dissociating it from the skyline beyond.

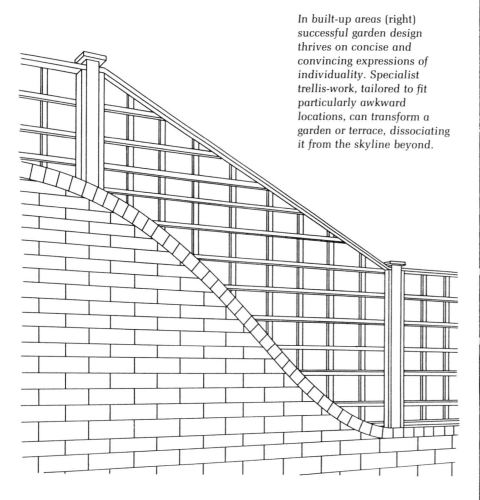

TAILORING AND EMBELLISHMENTS

The probability of off-the-shelf trellis having exactly the dimensions needed for a particular site is remote. This problem occurs most frequently along external walls and fence lines where trellis invariably has to start and finish at specific points. Thus carpentry is very often necessary for at least one panel.

Two principles should be remembered. The first is that the better the material and initial construction of the trellis, the easier it will be to indulge in amateur carpentry without weakening or spoiling the section that remains. Where the timbers are thin or heavily knotted, and the jointing is loose or minimal, the stress inflicted by on-site alterations can leave the finished article looking battle-weary before its job has begun. The strength and rigidity of some mass-produced trellis panels can depend on them remaining as a whole. Any subsequent reduction in their size may call for the addition of screws, both on internal joints and where they are fixed to uprights.

Secondly, where one panel has to be shorter than the others, with two uprights more closely spaced, try to site it where it is going to be least noticeable, so that it causes the minimum visual disruption to the rhythm of the overall plan. The further such a section is from a principle viewpoint, the better the results of any enforced modifications can be hidden. Alternatively, boundary trellising may run behind a tree or tall shrub which would provide convenient cover for an odd panel. Either way, calculate how much improvisation will be required and plan where it can best be inserted; then begin the installation of the trellis-work as far away as possible from that point, thus starting with the part where the visual impact is most critical and ending at the point where any modification or miscalculation can be best accommodated. In many gardens, the intended path of wall-top and boundary trellis is hindered by trees whose leaning trunks and branches cannot easily be removed. Carpentry may be necessary to cope with an obstruction and, as above, the stronger the grade and original construction of the trellis, the easier the whole operation. Two of the most disappointing and distracting sights are of trellis which looks crudely patched by on-site carpentry or a protruding trunk or limb squeezing through a gap with the air of a barely tolerated nuisance because the amount of trellis mesh removed has been so grudging. Try, instead, to make the most of what might otherwise be a visual black-spot. This may be an opportunity to try a rounded 'window', through which plant life in the form of a branch or trunk can pass on a completely different axis from the vertical of the lattice screen. Bizarre as such an approach may seem to the Western mind, the result can be unusually attractive. The proportions and flow of the trellis pattern are balanced and contrasted by the texture and line of the trunk, branch or stem.

Problems can also arise from leaning walls. Trellis looks awkward if it is tilting into or away from a garden; the answer to this problem is to use appropriately proportioned chocks or wall spacers between the uprights and the wall. This should make it possible to set the uprights, and therefore the trellis, on what appears to be the true vertical.

Chocks and wall spacers are also useful where the profile of a wall is broken by coping, cross-ribs, panels, piers and other embellishments set either proud or in recess. Notches can be chiselled out of uprights that have sufficient strength to tolerate the width of any protrusion, but this is not always possible with softwoods. Coping, especially, can be up to two or three inches proud of the walling below, demanding chocks or, if practical, the abandonment of side uprights in favour of sockets or brackets bolted straight into the top of the coping itself.

When erecting more than one panel of expanding diamond-mesh trellis, remember that the shape of the 'diamonds' is governed by the angle of the slats and therefore depends on the extent to which the complete section is expanded. If adjoining panels are not expanded to identical

dimensions, the pattern changes where they meet and appears confused.

If low-quality trellis is finished in a colourless or light stain, the tones of the wood are sometimes subject to marked and sudden variation due to different sources of timber being poorly matched. This seems more often the case with thin expanding trellises. Should one's intention be to cover it in heavy planting, the hint of a patch-work may not matter. Otherwise, it can be disappointing and distracting once erected. Where feasible, and preferably before erection, try a further finish, perhaps a stronger stain or a paint.

A cleverly scaled and beautifully restrained troupe l'oeil *with a figure of Neptune (opposite) makes a dramatic set-piece, with trellis carefully tailored to fit masonry and planting.*

These majestic trellised panels (below), in 'Repton blue', are off-set from both wall and paving, their diamond-mesh pattern embellished with circular niches and a bold framework of uprights, cross-pieces and rails.

SECURITY, INSURANCE AND THE LAW

Security

Most wall-top trellis helps to deter intruders (below); diamond and close-set meshes are generally less inviting to human climbers. Any damage to this wall from 'perils' (such as storms) could also involve an insurance claim in respect of the trellis as well, since the latter is employed as flat-to-wall decoration rather than 'fencing'.

Along the tops of boundary walls and fences, and around balconies and roof terraces, trellis-work can, generally, act as a moderately effective line of defence against intruders. Escape with household effects becomes that much more awkward. On the other hand, trellis cladding, on the flanks of house and boundary walls, might provide a useful toe-hold to those wishing to gain access to upper floors.

Some meshes and fixings can act as a greater encouragement than others to human climbers (including children trying to break out). Where square-mesh is sufficiently open in design to offer a good foothold, and sufficiently strong in construction and installation to carry considerable weight, the resulting structure can be used as a climbing frame. If security is a worry, the addition of sharply thorned roses or *Pyracantha* is a good idea.

Diamond-mesh is often seen as a more effective defence, being less comfortable to climb with ease; and any mesh, even if it is square-mesh, that is so dense as to inhibit any foothold at all will also be a deterrent. Poorly constructed or flimsy trellising, while representing a dubious investment in terms of the garden, can be infuriating to intruders hoping to make a discreet entry in that it snaps or fractures when subject to weight.

Insurance

All too frequently, trellis-work is subject to damage from more sudden perils than gradual wear and tear, some circumstances prompting enquiries to insurance companies as to whether a claim is possible. Most Building Insurance policies, at the outset, define the 'Building' as including both the residence and 'garages, outbuildings, landlord's fixtures and fittings, boundary and garden walls, gates, hedges and fences'. Thus, in principle, any trellising that forms a part of a boundary or fence, or that is attached to a building, is probably included. Also defined are the perils insured against (relevant to trellis-work) which normally include fire, explosion and earthquake, storm and flood, malicious persons, aerial devices or articles dropped therefrom, subsidence, ground heave and landslip, theft or any attempt thereat, impact by vehicles, horses and cattle, and falling trees.

However, most insurers, inevitably, insist on various exclusions which can directly affect claims on trellis-work. Storm damage to walls is covered, for instance, but not to gates and fences. Thus where there is trellis-work along the top of a wall and both suffer storm damage, the trellis might or might not be covered in the claim, depending upon whether it is seen as a fence or as part of the boundary wall. If such an issue arises, it should be explored

This stylish wall-top trellis (right) would effectively hamper the entry or escape of intruders. Unlike the panels illustrated opposite, this trellis may be categorized by some insurance underwriters as a 'fence' and, depending upon the circumstances, exclude it from their liabilities.

with one's broker or insurer. Trellis against walls, buildings and outbuildings is more immediately the basis of a storm damage claim. 'Falling trees' are usually qualified in that this must not be due to felling, lopping or topping, and must cause damage to more than gates and fences. Despite the exclusions and the excesses to which claims are subject, trellis and trellised structures are better covered under most insurance policies than is often realized.

The Law

There are various areas of the law that can affect trellis-work. Clear-cut guide-lines, however, are not always easy to establish because, while trellis is architectural in some senses and uses, it is also easily categorised as light-weight fencing.

The first concern is planning permission. If one lives in a listed building or conservation area, some trellised embellishments will require official consent. The substantial cladding of house walls (especially at the front), or conspicuous trellising around balconies or roof terraces, for instance, will change the appearance of the building. Other immediate attachments, such as a trellised porch or verandah, will also need permission. In the case of listed buildings

and conservation areas, furthermore, garden structures proposed within the curtilage of the house may be deemed to change the character of the property.

Free-standing trellised structures in the garden, otherwise, are unlikely to cause concern in most formats. A neighbour or planning officer may take issue where they are as large and prominent as was popular eighty years ago, or where, apart from size, they also incorporate doors, walls, windows and proper roofs. Curiosity may also be aroused where, as in a Lutyens-style pergola, a lot of structural brickwork is involved.

Boundary trellis tends to enjoy fairly wide parameters where it is categorized as a means of enclosure. If a judgement has to be made, the appropriate height is often seen as about six feet at the back of a property and three to four and a half feet where it fronts onto a highway. Where immediately adjacent to a highway, furthermore, its dimensions must not impair the 'sight-line' of passing traffic. In built-up areas, another issue is sometimes raised. Wall and fence-top trellis specifically, and garden structures generally, must not interfere with a neighbour's 'right of light'. To be on the safe side, all intending trellis builders should consult their local building regulations or zoning laws.

SUPPLIERS AND DESIGNERS

This directory contains a selective list of sources for trellis design and ready-made trellis. While every effort has been made to include as many sources as possible, the list should not be regarded as exhaustive. Every attempt has been made to ensure that the information given is correct, but the publishers cannot be held responsible for any inaccuracies.

UNITED KINGDOM

Andrew Crace Designs, 31 Bourne Lane, Much Hadham, Hertfordshire SG10 6ER   *Tel:* (027) 984 2685 *Fax:* (027) 984 3646
Trellis-work designs and details for furniture and garden buildings. Many styles available, including *chinoiserie*.

Artech, Unit 15, Burmarsh Workshops, Marsden Street, London NW5 3JA   *Tel:* (071) 482 2181 *Fax:* (071) 485 6030
Tailor-made wooden trellis-work, special commissions over a wide range of styles and some stock designs. *Treillage* a speciality.

Carter, Fulcher, Tate, Silverstone Farm, North Elmham, Norfolk NR2 0SEX   *Tel:* (0362) 818130
Neo-classical and *avant-garde* trellis-work designs and structures. Commission and some stock designs.

The Chelsea Gardener, 125 Sydney Street, London SW3   *Tel:* (071) 352 5656 *Fax:* (071) 352 3301
A 'shop window' for various craftsmen specializing in commissions and designs for *treillage, trompe-l'oeils*, trellised obelisks and other structures. The J. P. White Pyghtle Works catalogue (see p. 29) is one source of their designs.

Christopher Winder, Court Lodge Farm, Hinxhill, Ashford, Kent TN25 5NR   *Tel:* (0233) 625204 *Fax:* (0233) 621155
Tailor-made trellis-work in Swedish softwoods and English oak (from wind-blown trees). *Trompe-l'oeil* and gate designs a speciality.

Forest Glade, The Far Forest Works, Kidderminster, Worcestershire   *Tel:* (0229) 266203
Rustic styles for panels, arches and furniture, in peeled and treated oak. Stock designs and special commissions.

Hickson Timber Products Ltd., Castleford, West Yorkshire WF10 2JT   *Tel:* (0977) 556565 *Fax:* (0977) 516513
Special commissions and a wide range of structures and panels, both as stock designs and as individual modules for original composition. Hickson's originated and developed the treatment of timber that is now known as 'tannalising'.

HMP, Ditchford Farm, Morton in Marsh, Gloucestershire GL56 9RD   *Tel:* (0608) 62348 *Fax:* (0608) 63512
Steel trellis-work designs for arches, gazebos, bridges and other structures, many patterns taken from Victorian castings. Special commissions also undertaken.

Interior Trellis, Reed House, Mount Reed, Five Ashes, East Sussex TN20 6LN   *Tel:* (0825) 85766 *Fax:* (0825) 85216
Specialists in interior trellis-work with 40 different designs. All are offered as a standard range in pine, with beech, oak, mahogany and ash as options.

Jardine Leisure Furniture, Rosemount Tower, Wallington Square, Wallington, Surrey SM6 8RR   *Tel:* (081) 669 8265 *Fax:* (081) 669 8281
Trellised gazebo and matching furniture in fibre-glass, bonded with weather-proof marine resin.

Machin, Emerald Way, Stone Business Park, Stone, Staffordshire ST15 0SN   *Tel:* (0785) 818323 *Fax:* (0785) 814450
Stock designs and components (enabling individual composition) for trellised structures, panels and enclosures. Special emphasis on Classical and Gothic styles.

Mid-Wales Rustic, Llaithduu, Llandrindod Wells, Powys LD1 6YS   *Tel:* (059) 783 222 *Fax:* (059) 783 360
Rustic styles, in peeled and treated spruce, for arches, panels and furniture. Stock designs and special commissions.

Ollerton Engineering Services Ltd., Salmesbury Bottoms, Preston, Lancashire PR5 0RN   *Tel:* (025) 485 2127 *Fax:* (025) 485 4383
Galvanized steel structures (such as gazebos and pavilions) and furniture. Stock designs and special commissions.

Richard Sales, Garden Fitters, 48 Adelaide Terrace, Great West Road, Brentford TW8 9PQ   *Tel:* (081) 568 9162 *Fax:* (081) 550 9527
Specialist fitter of trellis and *treillage* in the garden.

Robin Eden, Pickwick End, Corsham, Wiltshire SN13 0JB *Tel:* (0249) 713335
One of the few suppliers of galvanized wire trellis-work with designs for arches, domes and furniture.

Shedlow Harrison's Joinery, Stratford St. Andrew, Saxmundham, Suffolk IP17 1LF *Tel:* (0728) 604264 *Fax:* (0728) 603162
Cast iron and iron wirework trellising for stock designs and special commissions. Gazebos and arches are a speciality.

Sheffield Architectural Metalworkers, 70 Westwick Crescent, Greenhill, Sheffield *Tel:* (0742) 376500
Trellis-work designs for primed steel arches.

Stuart Garden Architecture, Larchfield Estate, Dowlish Ford. Ilminster, Somerset TA19 0PF *Tel:* (0460) 57862 *Fax:* (0460) 53525
Trellis-work in stock designs and special commissions in all types of wood. *Treillage* a speciality.

Tiger Bridges, Milwards Farm, Laughton, Nr. Lewes, East Sussex BN8 6BN *Tel:* (032 183) 683
Specialists in bridges.

Thwaites and Pitt (Landscape Design) Ltd., 20 Bedford Court, Oakwood Lane, Roundhay, Leeds LS8 2PL *Tel:* (0532) 490658 *Fax:* (0532) 491454
A wide range of original patterns and styles for trellised panels and wall sculptures in wood. As well as stock designs, specific modules and components are also available for individual composition. Special commissions undertaken.

Trellisworks Ltd., Westmead, Clay Lane, Fishbourne, Chichester, West Sussex PO19 3JG *Tel:* (0243) 778566 *Fax:* (0243) 774238
Wooden trellis-work panels, structures and components in stock designs and as special commissions.

UNITED STATES AND CANADA

Bowbends, P.O. Box 900, Bolton, MA 01740 *Tel:* (508) 779 2271
Stock pieces and custom designs in cypress and yellow pine lattice-work for arches, gazebos, and other exotic garden structures. Ornamental bridges in Oriental, Chippendale and Germanic designs a speciality.

Country Casual, 17317 Germantown Road, Germantown, MD 20874 *Tel:* 1-800 872 8325 Freephone, (301) 540 0040 Maryland, (301) 428 3434 Metropolitan Washington D.C.
A superior collection of designer-styled and imported authentic designs from English custom workshops and joineries. A large selection of modular architectural *treillage*, solid teakwood site furnishings and garden seats.

Cumberland Woodcraft, P.O. Box 609, Carlisle, PA 17013 *Tel:* (717) 243 0063
Craftsmanship-quality reproductions of Victorian garden woodwork, including archways, finials, posts, brackets, moldings and beams for pavilions. Primarily of oak and poplar. Custom work gladly undertaken.

Dalton Pavilions, 7260 Oakley Street, Philadelphia, PA 19111 *Tel:* (215) 342 9804
Handcrafted and quality prefabricated gazebos and lattice-work garden structures made of select western red cedar.

Garden Concepts, 6621 Poplar Woods Circle South, Germantown, TN 38138 *Tel:* (901) 756 1649
Pre-assembled modules and units of teak and mahogany *treillage*. Designer specified styles.

Hickson Corporation, 1100 Johnson Ferry Road, Suite 680, Atlanta, Georgia 30342 *Tel:* (404) 843 2227.

Ivywood Gazebo, P.O. Box 9, Fairview Village, PA 19409 *Tel:* (215) 631 9104
A large variety of garden structures in red cedar, including lattice-work panels for fencing, and gazebos.

Machin Designs (USA) Inc., 557 Danbury Road (Route 7), Wilton, Connecticut 06897 *Tel:* (203) 834 9566.

New England Garden Ornaments, 38 East Brookfield Road, North Brookfield, MA 10535 *Tel:* (508) 867 4474
A unique resource for fine garden ornaments and architecture. Imported English trellis-work, as well as garden ornament, including garden houses, finials, balustrades, planters and cast-iron furniture.

Steptoe and Wife (Antiques) Ltd, 322 Geary Avenues, Toronto, Canada, M6H 2C7 *Tel:* (416) 530 4200

Stickney's, P.O. Box 34, One Thompson Square, Boston, MA 02129 *Tel:* (416) 242 1711 *Fax:* (617) 242 1982
Original designs and authentic replicas of classic garden structures of pink-grade mahogany. Palladian styles for small garden-houses, framing *treillage*, trellis and garden gates, and lattice-panel extensions.

Walpole Woodworkers, 767 East Street, Route 27, Walpole, MA 02081 *Tel:* (800) 343 6948
Custom designs and stock items of cedar lattice-work for arbours, fences and gates.

FRANCE	Barré-Bachelin, 21 Rue Marbeau, 75116 Paris *Tel:* (1) 45.00.98.11/45.00.60.72.
	Carré Neuf, 11 rue de Calais, 75009 Paris *Tel:* (1) 48.74.28.59.

FRANCE
Barré-Bachelin, 21 Rue Marbeau, 75116 Paris
Tel: (1) 45.00.98.11/45.00.60.72.

Carré Neuf, 11 rue de Calais, 75009 Paris
Tel: (1) 48.74.28.59.

Claustra Laudescher, z.i. de Pommenauque B.P. 165, 50500 Carentan
Tel: 33.42.09.52 *Fax:* 33.42.15.69.

GERMANY
Das Glashaus, 15 An der Eilshorts, D-2070 Grosshansdorf
Tel: (041) 02 61429 *Fax:* (041) 02 62420.

1001 – Otto Albert Lüghausen KG, D-500 Siegburg
Tel: (02241) 543 1001 *Fax:* (02241) 543 123.

Peters & Peters, Rugenbarg 51, D-2000 Hamburg-Norderstedt
Tel: (040) 5 23 40 93 *Telex:* 2 166 313 peped.

Teak and Garden, Gut Schönau, 2057 Reinbek-Ohe bei Hamburg
Tel: (041) 04 3033.

IRELAND
Irish Conservatories, The Naas Road, Bluebell, Dublin 12
Tel: (0001) 504183.

ITALY
Unopiu, S.S. Ortana Km 14,500, 01038 Soriana Nel Cimino (VT)   *Tel:* (0761) 759287/728166 *Fax:* (0761) 759288.

Also at Via Fratelli Bandiera 15, 20056 Trezzo D'Adda, Milan.

NETHERLANDS
Borg's Agenturen, Rijksstraatweg 725, 2245 CC Wassenaar
Tel: (01751) 76991.

SWITZERLAND
Hubert Houssin, Agency Laudescher, 74200 Thonon-les-Bains
Tel: 50.26.49.37 *Fax:* 50.26.06.29.

ACKNOWLEDGMENTS

The author and publisher wish to extend their special thanks to Gary St. John Newnes and to Kevin Thwaites for their generous and indefatigable help in the preparation of this book.

Thanks is also due to Peter Brook, Paul Kimche, Kenneth Medley, Angela McCann, Peter Richards and Roger Vickery.

PHOTOGRAPHY AND ILLUSTRATION CREDITS
All photographs in this book are by Hugh Palmer and all line illustrations by Annick Petersen, except the following: p. 4 Thames and Hudson p. 6 Thwaites and Pitt; pp. 8, 9 Artech; pp. 12, 14, Thames and Hudson; p. 15 Bibliothèque de l'Arsenale, Paris; pp. 16, 17, Thames and Hudson; pp. 20/21 Royal Horticultural Society; p. 21 Thames and Hudson; pp. 22/23 Royal Horticultural Society; pp. 24 (1), 24/25 Thames and Hudson; pp. 26, 27, 28, 29 (br) Royal Horticultural Society; pp. 30, 31 Thwaites and Pitt; p. 32 Artech; pp. 32/33, 33 Thwaites and Pitt; pp. 40/41 Artech; pp. 59 (br), 64 Jamie Garnock; p. 68 Thames and Hudson; p. 69 (ar) Artech; p. 73 (c and br) Jamie Garnock; p. 77 (b) Artech; p. 79 (a) Thames and Hudson; pp. 86, 90, 100 Thwaites and Pitt; pp. 102, 102/3, 112 Artech; p. 113 (a) Jamie Garnock; (b) Thwaites and Pitt; pp. 118, 119 Artech; pp. 120, 121 Jamie Garnock; pp. 122, 123 Artech; pp. 124, 125, 126, 127 Jamie Garnock; pp. 128/129, 133 (a), 140 (1), 143, 144, 145, Artech; p. 148 Jamie Garnock; p. 154 Artech; p. 155 Jamie Garnock. Plans on pp. 118/119, 122/123, 128/129 © Artech.

BIBLIOGRAPHY

Binney, Marcus and Hills, Anne, *Elysian Gardens*, London, 1979

Blondel, Jacques-François, *De la distribution des maisons de plaisance*, Paris, 1737

Brown, Jane, *The Art and Architecture of English Gardens*, London, 1989

Carter, Goode and Laurie, *Humphrey Repton*, London, 1982

Casa Valdes, Marquesa de, *Spanish Gardens*, Madrid, 1973 and London, 1987

Chambers, Sir William, *Designs for Chinese Buildings*, London, 1757

Chambers, Sir William, *Plans, Elevations, Sections, and Perspective Views of the Gardens and Buildings at Kew in Surrey*, London, 1763

Chambers, Sir William, *Dissertation on Oriental Gardening*, London, 1772

Chippendale, *The Gentlemen and Cabinetmaker's Director*, London, 1754

Conder, Josiah, *Landscape Gardening in Japan*, New York, 1893

Dezallier d'Argenville, Antoine-Joseph, *La théorie et la practique du jardinage*, Paris, 1709

Groen, J. van der, *Den Nederlandtsen Hovenier*, Leyden, 1669

Harvey, John, *Medieval Gardens*, London, 1981

Hayakawa, Masao, *The Garden Art of Japan*, New York, 1973

Hibberd, Shirley, *Rustic Adornments for Homes of Taste*, London, 1856

Hicks, David, *Garden Design*, London and Boston, 1982

Hill, Thomas, *Gardener's Labyrinth*, London, 1652

Hunt, John Dixon, *Garden and Grove*, London and Melbourne, 1986

Hunt, John Dixon and Willis, Peter, *The Genius of the Place*, Cambridge, Massachusetts and London, 1988

Huxley, Anthony, *Illustrated History of Gardening*, New York and London, 1978

Jacques, David and van der Horst, Arend Jan, *Gardens of William and Mary*, London, 1988

James, John, *The Theory and Practice of Gardening*, London, 1712 (a translation of D'Argenville's 1709 work)

Jekyll, Gertrude, *Garden Ornament*, London, 1918

Jekyll, Gertrude and Weaver, Sir Lawrence, *Gardens for Small Country Houses*, London, 1912

Jellicoe, Goode, Lancaster, *The Oxford Companion to Gardens*, Oxford and New York, 1986

Jones, Barbara, *Follies and Grottoes*, London, 1953 and 1974

Langley, Batty, *New Principles of Gardening*, London, 1728

Le Rouge, Georges Louis, *Détails des nouveaux jardins à la mode: jardins anglo-chinois*, Paris, 1776–87

Loudon, John Claudius, *Encyclopedia of Gardening*, London, 1822

Loudon, John Claudius, *Gardener's Magazine*, London, 1826–43

Loudon, John Claudius, *The Suburban Gardener and Villa Companion*, London, 1838

Manwaring, Robert, *The Cabinet and Chairmaker's Real Friend and Companion*, London, 1765

Mollet, André, *Le jardin de plaisir*, Paris, 1651

Mollet, Claude, *Théatre des plans et jardinages*, Paris, 1652

Morel, J.-M., *Théories des jardins*, Paris, 1776

Morris, Edwin T., *Gardens of China*, New York, 1983

Ottewill, David, *The Edwardian Garden*, New Haven and London, 1989

Over, Charles, *Ornamental Architecture in the Gothic Chinese and Modern Taste*, London, 1758

Papworth, John Buonarotti, *Hints on Ornamental Gardening: consisting of a series of designs for garden buildings etc.*, London, 1823

Plumptre, George and Garnock, Jamie, *Garden Ornament*, London and New York, 1989

Rea, John, *Flora, Ceres and Pomona*, London, 1665

Repton, Humphrey, *Sketches and Hints on Landscape Gardening*, London, 1795

Repton, Humphrey, *Observations on the Theory and Practice of Landscape Gardening*, London 1803

Repton, Humphrey, *Fragments on the Theory and Practice of Landscape Gardening*, 1816

Switzer, Stephen, *Ichnographia Rustica*, London, 1718

Temple, Sir William, *Upon the Gardens of Epicurus*, London, 1685

Thomas, Graham Stuart, *Recreating the Period Garden*, London, 1984

Thronger, Charles, *The Book of Garden Furniture*, London and New York, 1903

Triggs, Inigo, *Formal Gardens of England and Scotland*, London, 1902

Turner, Tom, *English Garden Design*, London, 1986

Van Oosten, Hendrik, *De Nieuwe en Naaukeurige Nederlandse Hovenier*, Leyden, 1716

Verey, Rosemary, *Classic Garden Design*, London, 1984

White, J. P., *Pyghtle Works Catalogues*, Bedford, early twentieth century

Wise, George and Henry, *The Retired Gardener*, London, 1717

Wise, George and Henry, *The Complete Gardener*, London, 1717

Woodbridge, Kenneth, *Princely Gardens*, London, 1986

INDEX